Accounts Payable

Accounts Payable

A Guide to Running an Efficient Department

2003 Cumulative Supplement

Mary S. Ludwig Schaeffer
Editor of IOMA's Report on Managing Accounts Payable

WILEY
John Wiley & Sons, Inc.

This book is printed on acid-free paper. ∞

Copyright © 2003 by Mary S. Schaeffer and the Institute of Management Administration. All rights reserved.

Published by John Wiley & Sons, Inc., Hoboken, New Jersey
Published simultaneously in Canada.

For general information on our other products and services or for technical support, please contact our Customer Care Department within the United States at (800) 762-2974, outside the United States at (317) 572-3993 or fax (317) 572-4002.

Wiley also publishes its books in a variety of electronic formats. Some content that appears in print may not be available in electronic books.

For more information about Wiley products, visit our web site at www.wiley.com.

Library of Congress Cataloging-in-Publication Data:

Ludwig Schaeffer, Mary S.
    Accounts payable : a guide to running an efficient department / Mary S. Ludwig Schaeffer.
        p.   cm.
    Includes bibliographical references and index.
    ISBN 0-471-29857-3 (cloth : alk. paper)
    ISBN 0-471-46473-2 (supplement)
    1. Accounts payable.   I. Title.
HF5681.A27L83   1999
658.8'8—DC21   98-28232
                                                                              CIP

Printed in the United States of America

10 9 8 7 6 5 4 3 2 1

for
Richard Mark Guillen,
a young man who brought joy
to everyone he met

Update Service

BECOME A SUBSCRIBER!
Did you purchase this product from a bookstore?

If you did, it's important for you to become a subscriber. John Wiley & Sons, Inc. may publish, on a periodic basis, supplements and new editions to reflect the latest changes in the subject matter that you *need to know* in order to stay competitive in this ever-changing industry. By contacting the Wiley office nearest you, you'll receive any current update at no additional charge. In addition, you'll receive future updates and revised or related volumes on a 30-day examination review.

If you purchased this product directly from John Wiley & Sons, Inc., we have already recorded your subscription for this update service.

To become a subscriber, please call **1-877-762-2974** or send your name, company name (if applicable), address, and the title of the product to:

mailing address:	**Supplement Department** **John Wiley & Sons, Inc.** **One Wiley Drive** **Somerset, NJ 08875**
e-mail:	**subscriber@wiley.com**
fax:	**1-732-302-2300**
online:	**www.wiley.com**

For customers outside the United States, please contact the Wiley office nearest you:

Professional & Reference Division
John Wiley & Sons Canada, Ltd.
22 Worcester Road
Etobicoke, Ontario M9W 1L1
CANADA
Phone: 416-236-4433
Phone: 1-800-567-4797
Fax: 416-236-4447
Email: canada@wiley.com

John Wiley & Sons Australia, Ltd.
33 Park Road
P.O. Box 1226
Milton, Queensland 4064
AUSTRALIA
Phone: 61-7-3859-9755
Fax: 61-7-3859-9715
Email: brisbane@johnwiley.com.au

John Wiley & Sons, Ltd.
The Atrium
Southern Gate, Chichester
West Sussex PO 19 8SQ
ENGLAND
Phone: 44-1243-779777
Fax: 44-1243-775878
Email: customer@wiley.co.uk

John Wiley & Sons (Asia) Pte., Ltd.
2 Clementi Loop #02-01
SINGAPORE 129809
Phone: 65-64632400
Fax: 65-64634604/5/6
Customer Service: 65-64604280
Email: enquiry@wiley.com.sg

Supplement Contents

Note to the Reader: Sections not in the main bound volume are indicated by "(New)" after the title. Material new to *this* supplement is indicated by an asterisk (*) in the left margin in the contents and throughout the supplement.

Supplement Contents

Supplement Contents

Supplement Contents

Supplement Contents

Supplement Contents

Preface

The accounts payable world is evolving from a poorly thought of manual arena into a smooth, high-tech world. While the number of people employed in the profession will decrease, those that remain will be savvy, innovative women and men with sharp analytical skills. They will be the people who are able to change and who are not afraid of the unknown. Techniques that were considered leading-edge just a few short years ago have quickly moved down the ladder—first considered a best practice and now just an everyday approach. The biggest changes involve the move from the manual, paper-intensive, clerical process to one that is technology-driven and analytical. Companies are adopting e-invoicing. P-cards and e-mail are everywhere.

This does not mean that some of the old tried-and-true practices can't be tweaked and don't still have a place in the accounts payable department of the future. To that end, we've added information in this supplement on using statements, filing, 1099s, Sales and Use Tax, defenses against check fraud, and much more.

One of the really fascinating changes is the way duplicate-payment audits are evolving. Technology has made the traditional third-party duplicate-pay audit less popular, but that does not mean that the firms are going away. In an interview with representatives from seven firms, we take a look into the future. These firms are looking to take the audit to the next step—many are offering other services, and some are now looking at contract compliance audits.

Companies are still interested in benchmarking, with a growing number looking for innovative ways to benchmark their own accounts payable departments. Interviews and case studies of several successful metric-based operations are included.

Accounts payable professionals are continuing to find innovative ways to use the Internet. Use of e-mail is just the beginning. Included in this supplement are the results of a recent survey showing the numerous ways accounts payable associates at companies of all sizes are using the Internet. Their ingenuity will surprise you.

One of the most interesting features in this supplement is the case studies, featuring a myriad of companies that are taking advantage of and utilizing the latest technology to improve their operations and develop a paperless accounts payable department. Okay, that might be overstating the case, but the reality is that paper is finally being reduced in accounts payable departments. Read the numerous case studies about the innovative professionals who have found ways to implement the accounts payable departments of the future without spending a fortune.

We end with an outsourcing tale—one that will appeal to most accounts payable associates but not necessarily outsourcers. It is a tale of a company that outsourced its accounts payable department and wasn't pleased with the outcome, so a savvy manager un-outsourced the work.

These are demanding times for workers everywhere, and those in the accounts payable profession may be challenged more than some in more established professions. The new tools and techniques discussed in this book will help them meet those challenges, or should we say, opportunities. I wish the best of luck.

MARY S. SCHAEFFER

February 12, 2003

Part One

Traditional Functions

1

Invoice Handling

p. 5. Add new section:

1.2A   BLANKET PURCHASE ORDERS (NEW)

When it comes to blanket purchase orders (POs), accounts payable professionals either love them or hate them. There seems to be no middle ground. Payables and purchasing managers like them for places from which they buy many times a month to streamline the process. Others dislike them because of the lack of control. Blanket POs cover multiple orders and shipments. Typically, they are used for repetitive purchases. Either way, all seem to have strong opinions. Here is what our subscribers have to say about them:

Jay S. Wood of GTE Worldwide Telecommunications uses blanket POs extensively. Wood notes though that due to the manner in which blankets are established, verification of receipt for goods and services remains a manual process. Wood also notes that they issued uncommitted blankets, but they do not commit those funds to the vendor. The blanket can be closed, reduced, or upgraded at any time.

The funds on the blanket are similar to funds in a checking account. They are there to pay the vendor, but GTE can discontinue the relationship with the vendor at any time and close the blanket—hence, the reason the funds are uncommitted to the vendor. On some occasions, Wood said, they "issue committed funds for a particular vendor, when we contract with the vendor for a particular service or supply at a preset price."

Any invoice received against a blanket PO requires an approval and verification from an authorized individual responsible for the goods or services on the PO. Added Wood, "Once they approve the invoice, we process it and decrement the PO. Each PO has a life of one year, if it is not canceled sooner. Funds can be added to extend the life of the blanket, so long as it has not expired. We use blanket POs for such things as office supplies, equipment leases, office cleaning, and maintenance, etc."

Vicki Lindsey, accounts payable manager of RPC, Inc., is another admirer. "We use blanket purchase orders for places that we buy from many times during a month. We give the vendor a purchase order number at the beginning of the month and tell him everything we buy through the last day of the month should have that number. At the beginning of every month the vendors call us for a new purchase number. When our people pick up the merchandise during the month they bring a delivery ticket back with them. We attach it to the purchase order and when the invoice arrives we simply match it with all the delivery tickets. Works well for us, we've done this for many years. You can also do weekly purchase orders, if preferred."

An anonymous accounts payable manager from Chicago does not seem to agree. "I think they're a dumb idea! They simply tell a vendor that someone may order up to some amount from you but often there are no controls in place to check to see whether expenditures are adding up to or exceeding the approved amount. Purchasing people like them because they think it helps control expenditures. All it does is create paperwork."

As can be seen from these radically different points of view, blanket POs can work in some organizations but are not without their own inherent problems (i.e., the control issues). Review your own operations before deciding if blanket POs will work in your organization.

p. 7. Insert new section:

1.4A   WHEN A/P GETS INVOICES LAST (NEW)

Whether invoices should all be sent first to accounts payable and then to the person who needs to authorize the transaction, or vice versa, is a debated issue. The traditional view is that if the invoices come to accounts payable first, the department can then track the invoices and follow up when they are not returned in a timely manner for payment. But why should accounts payable have to spend its time making sure others do what they are supposed to do?

(a)   Changing Philosophies

A small, but growing, number of companies are shying away from the traditional route and insisting that other departments handle their own invoice processing responsibilities without the accounts payable department overseeing their workflow. When this happens, accounts payable often gets invoices late, long after the company has any reasonable chance of qualifying for an early payment discount. Worse, the invoice frequently gets lost and when vendors call accounts payable looking for payment, they are told the invoice was never received and another copy should be sent. Ultimately, in some companies, both copies end up being paid.

There is some hope on the horizon, thanks in part to technology, which is playing a big role in the changes in accounts payable. In those instances where invoices are received electronically, it almost doesn't matter who gets them first as they can be forwarded effortlessly. With online lookup capabilities, everyone can check.

(b)   Order of Business

Although accounts payable would like to receive invoices first, this procedure is no longer followed by many companies. Either a new accounting system is installed or a change in corporate philosophy requires the change. Whatever the reason, accounts payable professionals should insist that the following procedures be instituted should their company take the accounts-payable-last route.

- Vendors should be supplied with new bill-to addresses that reflect the name and/or the department of the authorizer.
- Calls about payment status should be referred to the authorizer unless there is a good online tracking system.
- Even with a good online tracking system, payment calls may still be routed to the authorizer as accounts payable may be able only to tell the caller if a payment is scheduled, not why it has or has not been scheduled.
- Other departments must understand and fully accept their responsibilities in regard to vendor payment and stop blaming payment delays on accounts payable.
- Ongoing communication between accounts payable and approving departments is essential.

(c)   Closing Thoughts

Don't be surprised to find some resistance to an accounts-payable-last change. Other departments may not want accounts payable to get invoices last; many like the comfort of having accounts payable keeping track of payments for them.

p. 10. Add the following new section after carryover paragraph:

1.8A   STRATEGIES TO USE WHEN SHORT-PAYING INVOICES (NEW)

Accounts payable managers often pay an invoice for less than the amount on the original invoice. They take a discount if the invoice is paid early and make deductions for short shipments, defective goods, promotional programs, or a variety of other reasons. The result of these actions is another phone call into the accounts payable department, requiring research time to determine the reason for the short-pay. When these phone calls are added to the already overworked accounts payable staff, the workload threatens even the most dedicated members. However, there are great solutions to this problem. Several accounts payable professionals have found techniques to eliminate this phone call by a letter or debit memo just saying "No."

(a)   Letter

The simplest way to handle short-pays is to include a letter along with the payment explaining why the invoice was paid short. Accounts payable professionals who use this approach success-fully use a form letter. The letter contains a long list of common reasons for short-paying an invoice and the accounts payable pro-fessional simply checks off the appropriate box. These letters also typically include several lines where someone can add the appro-priate comments.

Those who use this letter are advised to keep copies of them. That is because collection managers who do not agree with the conclusions are likely to call to argue their cases. Having the let-ter readily at one's disposal will make handling of such calls much easier.

(b)   Debit Memo

"I am wondering," writes one manager on the IOMA accounts payable discussion group, "if I'm the only accounts payable manager who requires debit memos for payment deductions taken on invoices. Some accounts payable departments don't think there is any added value to create a debit memo for simple deductions. They mark through the original invoice amount and write in the amount to pay." The responses to this query indicate that by far this professional is not alone in his approach. Here's what a few other accounts payable professionals had to say about this approach:

- You are not the only one using this procedure. Many accounts payable managers require it. As a consultant in accounts payable systems for many years, I have seen this problem attacked both ways. Tracing and auditing prob-lems are found more often when the face of the invoice is adjusted. This is a hidden correction and can create additional work for both you and the vendor. The debit memo route offers more control and is less work in the long run. The full amount of the invoice should be paid, and the amount of discrepancy should be deducted via a debit memo.

This is especially true if you are matching invoice amounts in your duplicate payment controls. If the invoice is paid once at the adjusted amount and another time at the full amount, it will not be detected by duplicate payment software. Also, you can immediately see those vendors who are overcharging and take steps to correct it. The easy way is not always the best way. You are doing it the correct way.

- I have been using debit memos for years to both record the deduction as a separate transaction and use it as the vehicle for notifying the vendor of the issue. Sometimes it is difficult to have a staff change from one mode of operation to another but, given time, the realization will come that this saves a lot of time and phone calls. When the vendor responds, if the debit memo has been descriptive, they will have answers or at least knowledge of the issue and will be more ready to discuss in an informed manner.

- No! You are not alone. When I started at a new company last year, I found that they were paying invoices short. The research time was unbelievable. After vendors called, we researched, told them the invoice was paid, why it was paid short, and then we did it again and again and again. We developed a debit memo system in Access™. Now we get the form to send to the vendor and the report for the reconciliation staff, as well as easier research. We have saved four hours a week researching.

- It is hard to imagine anybody not using the debit memo system. There have been times when an invoice slips by me with the amount changed, and I certainly get phone calls. It seems that is just asking for more work.

(c)   Just Say NO!

A small group takes the view that no invoice should be paid until it is prepared correctly. This group of accounts payable professionals is well aware that any time an invoice is not paid for the original amount, but manually changed, the odds of a duplicate payment increase tremendously. Rather than put their companies at risk, they require an original corrected invoice.

One professional explains why her company went from the debit memo route to requiring a corrected invoice. "We used to use debit memos, but found that changing the vendor's invoice, even with a debit memo, didn't work well. We still ended up researching deductions or changes, because the vendor would still call and question the debit memo! Instead, we established a policy of never short-paying a vendor invoice. We make one exception—that of sales tax deductions." (For which a notice accompanies the check to explain the deduction and offers the vendor a point of contact to obtain a copy of the resale certificate if necessary.)

"Since we won't short-pay an invoice, we require the vendor to issue a credit and rebill before we will pay anything on the entire invoice," she continued. "In the long run, we found requests to research short payments were completely eliminated. Our monthly statements were clean and our accounts almost never have past-due balances that need to be researched."

By refusing to short-pay the bill, you require the vendor to update its system so that those collection efforts for remaining balances are eliminated. You also reinforce the fact that you will not tolerate billing errors. The quickest way to eliminate poor-quality work is to refuse to accept it in the first place. Make the vendors fix their own errors, and they will soon learn not to make them anymore. If they want to be paid, they will make the adjustments you require.

(d)   What These Techniques Do

Good communication with regard to short-pay is essential. Communicate with your vendors and let them know exactly why you are not paying the entire invoice. Although this takes a little extra effort, you will be paid back many times over by the reduction in phone calls and work associated with researching why an invoice was not paid in full. It should be noted that these techniques will not completely eliminate the phone calls. These approaches merely get rid of the inquiry calls and the research work associated with those calls. The "discussions" with the suppliers over the appropriateness of those deductions will not be obliterated.

Clearly, each of these techniques will not work in all organizations. Obviously, you are not going to threaten not paying a bill should a key supplier not redo its invoice. It takes time and effort to make these processes work. However, this will pay off in the long run as the calls decrease and the time saved doing research is put to better use. Make the short-term investment of your time and reap the long-term rewards.

p. 12. Insert new sections:

1.13A HOW TO KEEP DIFFICULT INVOICES FROM DISAPPEARING (NEW)

Whenever an organization finds itself inundated with paper, some of it is bound to get lost in the shuffle. This is especially true if that paper requires action to be taken and the appropriate response is not quite clear. Accounts payable professionals handling difficult invoices fall into this group. Many accounts payable managers complain that invoices have a way of disappearing into "never-never" land. This issue was the subject of hot discussion on the IOMA discussion group recently. "We have recently discovered that some of our accounts payable desks had some buried issues hidden in them," writes one harried manager. Some of the items included: debit memos not taken, returned checks, and old invoices. "We have been considering auditing desks within our department every month to ensure that buried issues do not go unnoticed. Does anyone have any other methods that are less intrusive to ensure that these issues do not pile up?" the manager concludes.

(a)   Recommendations

- Rotate desk assignments every six months or so. It helps improve training and backup, prevent fraud, and brings a lot of potential problems to the light of day.

- Have an invoice amnesty day! With no questions asked, allow staffers to return all "problem invoices, etc." to the manager. If there are no repercussions, staffers will feel free to return work they do not know how to handle.

- Maintain a database of discrepant invoices. When it becomes apparent that the invoice is discrepant, the processor can create an e-mail that is sent to the buyer. This serves two purposes; we know what kind of hidden liability we have out there and it requires purchasing to take ownership of the problem. The processor then files the invoice in a discrepant file until the buyer e-mails back that the invoice is "repaired" and ready for payment. This allows the processor to "transfer" responsibility and keeps the invoices out of the black hole. Processors are also required to register their backlog each week. Obviously, if the processors did not comply, there would be a problem.

- Spring cleaning. Unfortunately, there is no method more effective than actually cleaning out a desk in someone's absence. Although it is embarrassing at times, the point is nailed home. Some accounts payable clerks have a penchant for hiding problems and thinking they are resolved by keeping them out of sight. The desks, invoices, credit memos, statements, and related documents are company property and available for review. Allow each person to have one drawer for personal use and NEVER get in that drawer.

- Set up the desks uniformly—one place for statements, one place for problem invoices, one place for credit memos, and so on. You can tell at a glance where someone is just by looking at his or her desktop. This encourages the clerks to keep current.

(b)   Conclusion

One accounts payable professional relayed a humorous anecdote about this issue. "I had an accounts payable clerk (one of my best) tell me that she thought the rummaging of desks was intrusive, demeaning, and totally unnecessary. I eventually promoted her to accounts payable manager. One of the first things she did was inspect the desks once she found out how many items were being hidden." Also, the same clerk mentioned above told me, "There is no such thing as 'pending items.'" All that means is that nothing is getting done about the problem. Delete the "pending" file.

Before going through employees' drawers on a regular basis, consult your boss and the human resources department. As an added precaution, it might not be a bad idea to have someone with you in case there is a problem later on.

Once again, accounts payable professionals have found innovative solutions to handle the pesky problems that make running the department such a challenge.

* 1.13B   STATEMENTS: A/P CAN IMPACT THE BOTTOM LINE BY CORRECTLY UTILIZING VENDOR STATEMENTS (NEW)

Vendor statements can be useful tools for accounts payable professionals, if used correctly. Used improperly, they can lead to duplicate payments—definitely not a desirable outcome. Given the controversy and accounts payable interest that surrounds their use, here's a review of best vendor statement practices, as well as commentary from accounts payable professionals who use vendor statements on a regular basis.

(a)   Best A/P Practices

"Never pay from statements" is the mantra in many accounts payable departments. The reasoning for this stance is that statements often contain invoices that have been paid or that have been issued and possibly mailed but not cashed.

There is one variation to the never-pay-from-statements best practice. This occurs with those vendors that send numerous small-dollar invoices to the company. Typical examples might include overnight delivery services, messenger services, and so on. In these cases, some companies have decided to pay only from statements. Once a month, or week, or whatever time period is appropriate, the vendor sends a statement and the company pays it. Any invoices received from statement vendors are discarded. Vendors whose payments are based on statements are never paid from an invoice.

The other best practice regarding the use of vendor statements is to periodically request a vendor statement showing all activity. In this manner, the accounts payable professional can identify any outstanding credits. Many suppliers do not list credits on their statements unless specifically requested to include them. And, if your company doesn't know about a credit, it is unlikely to utilize it.

(b)   In Reality

The question of how other accounts payable professionals use vendor statements was raised on the IOMA accounts payable discussion group (*www.ioma.com/forum/*) Here's a sampling of the comments:

- *Our company reconciles vendor statements.* This makes us aware of any discrepancies on our account. Sometimes invoices never reach the accounts payable department. If we do not have an invoice that is listed on the statement, we call and request a copy. Also, the statement will show a credit balance if a duplicate payment is made. Reconciling vendor statements has always been a useful tool in our department.

- *We review statements for any items over 30 days old.* We assume anything less than 30 days crossed in the mail. Any invoices over 30 days not in our system, we call for copies.

- *My company is on the Evaluated Receipt System, also known as "pay-on-receipt."* As a result, my staff does not look at any invoices. What we do instead is target 100 of our largest and/or most strategic suppliers and reconcile these statements on a rotating schedule of 50 per quarter. We also reconcile other suppliers as the need arises. One thing we have found is that some suppliers send a "statement" of only the outstanding invoices. No overpayments of cash on account items are listed. What we request now is an "ageing" of our account, and this usually lists all open items. We have found many outstanding credits this way.

- *It is very important to reconcile statements.* There could be invoices lost in the mail. Unless you look at the statement, how do you know? If this process is very cumbersome, divide the volume among accounts payable staff.

- *We review items over 45 days old.* At the end of each year we also request statements from our top 25 vendors by both dollar volume and transaction volume. These are reconciled and reviewed for credits.

- *We review our vendor statements regularly.* During our busy season, we don't always look at every single one, but it is a department requirement to have them all reconciled at the end of the year.

- *We review statements.* It helps with the relationship and resolving issues.

As can be seen from the preceding commentary, reviewing statements is a worthwhile task and can pay big dividends when previously unknown credits surface. Identifying these items is one way that accounts payable can make a positive impact on the bottom line.

* 1.13C   FILING: ADVOCATES OF BATCH FILING SQUARE OFF AGAINST THE ALPHA PROPONENTS (NEW)

The need to quickly and easily research invoices, as well as route, pull vouchers with special attachments, and handle remittance stubs, all build off a process that can make or break your department. Ultimately, how you handle the process essentially boils down to whether you want to use a batch or alpha filing system. To get a perspective on which is better, we turned to the discussion raging on the accounts payable chat group, at *www.ioma.com/forum*.

(a)   The Problem

Here's how one pro described the problem at her company: "We currently file invoices (with check copies attached) by vendor. Our filing falls behind quite often and then our analysts spend a lot of time trying to find things that aren't yet filed. I would like to switch to batch filing for next year and would like to hear the pros and cons of each approach. Our intent is that we would no longer print check copies or match the invoices to the check copies. As soon as checks come out, they would be forwarded to the mailroom for mailing." Additionally, she wanted to know:

1. How did you implement the switch to batch filing?
2. When/how is data entry reviewed?
3. How do you store the batches (e.g., in folders, in envelopes, etc.)?
4. How do you handle remittance stubs? ("We don't return all remittance stubs but we've found that, because we have so many different phone and utility accounts, it saves headaches in the long run if we return the stubs for our phone and utility vendors.")
5. How do you handle checks that need to be routed to someone within your organization or that need to be sent via overnight delivery? ("If we're no longer matching invoices with checks we won't see the sticker on the invoice indicating any special instructions.")
6. For 4 and 5, do you pull out from the batches any vouchers with remit stubs/special instructions so they can be handled individually when the checks are cut?

This is the essence of the problem as experienced at many firms.

(b) Success Story #1

"We implemented batch filing several years ago, when we went live with Oracle," responded another accounts payable manager. She answered the questions raised in the previous section as follows:

1. "Since Oracle provided an input screen for batch information it provided the controls we were looking for."
2. "We have three auditors, who did a 15 percent manual audit, after the fact. We implemented an Imaging & Workflow system last year, which automated this process."
3. "We developed batch-naming standards and created batch cover sheets. We then filed them by batch name."
4. "Since we print remittance information on our checks, we only have to allow for exceptions. We created a database for special delivery instructions. Our support staff ensures these are handled appropriately. As for utilities (specifically phones), we remove the remittance stub before the batch is filed. The stubs are given to our support person, who matches them to the phone checks (we have the capability to sort draft types, so they don't have to look through all the drafts)."
5. "Again, this is where we use the database. The processor enters details into the database, then the support person reviews the database for special instructions when handling the drafts."

"We use the Priority Code field. We have set up several different codes to sort various types of drafts together. This can be done at the vendor or invoice level. There is no report; but due to the types of payments we sort, it is quite easy for the person to tell where one set stops and the next starts. As for our database, it is a simple form completed by the processor; the person doing the drafts reviews it each morning to see what to pull and where to send it. This adds a second checkpoint, in case the priority code was not correct."

(c)   Success Story #2

Here's what a second advocate of batch filing had to say: "Even if you are filing by batches, it is easier to go and search a folder or envelope than when they are filed alphabetically.

"Here is how we handle remittances and *special checks*: We remove the stub as we key in the invoice. We create numbered plastic tags. Every technician gets a different color tag sequence. We attach a tag to the envelop with the remittance; we also have a field in our database where we key in this number. As we print the check, this number is printed as well so we know that there is an envelope already. This way we don't have to run any special reports to match remittance to the checks.

"As far as the batch filing goes, we don't file anything. Every week we send out our batches for imaging and store everything on CD. The original is stored at an off-site location. Very seldom do we need to request a batch to be brought back. Every piece of information is on CD. The cost is money well spent. Until you have this capability, just file everything by batch number. I suggest that you attach a report on the outside of your folders to show you what's inside."

(d)   An Endorsement

"I don't believe it," chimed in a third professional. "If you batch with a manageable number of transactions—20 to 25—and make sure the batch reference is on the folder, as well as available online (your inquiry screens), you can't go wrong. If someone calls in with a query, always use your system first (that's why we have systems); if you need to retrieve the invoice, your system notates the batch reference, and you then have to flick through 20 to 25 invoices to find it. Searching by alpha means that instead of 20 to 25 invoices, you may have to search through hundreds. Plus you have the long-winded process of filing."

In the batch-versus-alpha battle, alpha never wins, concludes this manager.

(e)   A Ringing Denouncement

To put it mildly, this next gentleman, an experienced accounts payable professional who just started a new position at a company that uses a batch filing system, does not agree: "This is a hot topic for me," he writes. He says that in comparison to the two other companies, which filed alphabetically, he thinks batch-filing systems are awful.

"From a management perspective, it looks like a great idea because you just dump the files into the file cabinet by date order and forget about them, supposedly freeing up the accounts payable assistants to do other tasks. Seems simple, right? Wrong. What it really does is create a vast amount of work on the back end for both finance employees and auditors. Got a problem with a duplicate invoice? Instead of pulling one or two files, you have to waste tons of valuable time pulling single invoices from scattered file drawers. Then some unlucky accounts payable assistant has to spend even more time refiling all of the invoices that were pulled. It's even worse when you're going through an audit.

"Have to do a manual check? (Nobody does those, right?) Where do you file it: under the date or in voucher order? I'm looking right now at a large pile of manual checks that no one has filed because they're out of sequence and need to be placed in separate folders. What a mess. This problem is compounded when you have independent offices in other cities.

"Batch processing doesn't save time," he concludes, "it wastes vast amounts of it. My suggestion would be to create a more efficient alphabetical filing system, like having your accounts payable assistants file their invoices every day instead of letting them pile up. Or, if you are organized and can afford it, try an imaging system."

After reading some of the responses to his comments, this gentleman added the following to his remarks: "In response to the people who disagreed with me regarding alpha versus batch filing, I don't believe you addressed the fundamental issues I brought up. Despite all of the propaganda about how great batch filing is and how easy it is to look everything up, the system definitely has flaws. For example, suppose FedEx is bugging you about an invoice that wasn't paid from a previous month. Sure, the first thing you would do is look it up in the system. This is obvious—I think we all do that anyway—but that doesn't finish the job because the vendor will probably want a copy of the check, and you probably want to research it anyway to make sure it wasn't already paid.

"So you have to search by date, or batch reference number, search drawers, and pull the check out of a pile of unrelated invoices. This gives you no background on the vendor or the check. What if there was a double payment? People who use batch filing will never know, because they can't see an accurate invoice history in their systems *or* in the file drawers. You completely lose one component of your ability to research an invoice. It was also mentioned that 'searching by alpha means that instead of 20 to 25 invoices you may have to search through hundreds.' This isn't true. If you know the vendor name and the check number (the checks should be filed numerically by check number in your vendor file anyway), you should be able to find the invoice (plus any related invoices or correspondence) immediately. Plus, if a check is misfiled, it's easy to find as opposed to the batch filing system where you may never see it again!

"Finally, it was remarked, 'Plus you have the long-winded process of filing,' to which I reply, '*You* have the long-winded process of researching problems.' Auditors or A/P assistants can easily pull history on a whole vendor instead of having to search through file drawers or call up multiple boxes from archives.

"As I said before, sure, it's easy to just dump your invoices in a file drawer and forget about them, but doing so usually comes back to bite you down the road. The time it takes to file alphabetically is really exaggerated (unless you're disorganized) because your checks should print alphabetically anyway. Besides, an accounts payable clerk who files invoices will have a much better idea of what's really going on with his or her vendors."

He concluded, "In my view, batch filing is for you if speed is the most important factor for you, and you can live with a confusing and potentially sloppy system. Alphabetical filing, on the other hand, is more thorough, accurate, and easily researched."

(f) Two Others Board the Alpha Wagon

The accounts payable professional quoted in the previous section was not alone in his dislike of batch filing. Here's what two other professionals had to say about the process:

> We considered the batch process, but knew in the long run that filing the invoices back in the correct batch would be time-consuming. Our checks come off the system in alphabetical order so the filing doesn't take too long and it is done weekly. Our miscellaneous folder for each letter of the alphabet is also filed alphabetically within itself. This way, when you have five paid invoices, a new folder is made for that vendor. We have various people who need groups of invoices paid for the same vendor, and with vendor filing, they just go to that vendor's file. Fortunately, we do have a volunteer to come in to do the filing. But, when she is out, it falls back onto me. Batch filing is not for us.

> I never liked batch filing when research is required on one particular vendor. What is easier when investigating 1099 information or during a state or IRS audit: locate the one file with all the invoices, or locate multiple batches? After 15 years in accounts payable, I'll vote for one centralized file location any day.

Each company has to make its own decision based on its requirements and priorities. The professionals who took the time to share their experiences have provided the accounts payable community with the information they need to make the alpha-versus-batch decision for their own organizations.

2

Check Preparation, Printing, and Filing

p. 22. Insert following carryover material at top of page:

2.2A   AUTHORIZED SIGNERS (NEW)

The approval process is filled with problems. For starters, one has to know who can approve what. Then there is the issue of verifying the signatures on the invoices, purchase orders, and check requests to make sure that the signature on the document is accurate. One of the easiest ways for an employee to perpetrate internal fraud is to simply fill out a check request and sign the boss's name to the request. If the company has good internal controls (which include never returning the check to the original requester but simply mailing it to the payee), the process would actually help the underling perpetrate the fraud.

(a)   List of Approvers

To address these issues, companies should develop a list of authorized approvers and a detailed listing of the levels of approval. While this listing should be available to those who need the information—specifically the people in accounts payable preparing the payments and the internal audit staff—it should not be readily accessible. Similarly, while approvers or signers need to know their own limits, they do not need to know the limits of everyone else in the company.

The listings of approvers and their limits should be kept in a secure place. It should be given only to those who need this information and should never be left lying around. Some companies have put this information on their intranet sites and have password limits on who can access it.

(b)   Signature Cards

To make sure that the right person is signing or approving the documentation, companies should keep copies of the signatures on file. Traditionally, these were kept on signature cards similar to those used by banks to verify signatures. Many an accounts payable professional can recount tales of senior executives, with exceedingly sloppy handwriting under normal circumstances, using the utmost care to fill out the signature card for the official company records. The result of their care is that the signature on the card bears no resemblance to the scrawl they normally put on documents to approve payments. So when these cards are given to the approvers, they should be told to sign them as they would any other document—in their usual illegible scrawl. Otherwise, the documents they approve for payment will be bounced.

(c)   Signature Cards in the Twenty-First Century

Like every other facet of accounts payable, technology is making inroads into approval lists and signature cards. "I would like to know what companies are doing to verify appropriate authorization signatures. Lists, signature cards, or something else?" wrote one inquisitive accounts payable professional on the Institute of Management and Administration (IOMA) Accounts Payable discussion group at *www.ioma.com.* Here is what two innovators had to say:

- Our company has built an online Lotus Notes™ tool that provides two functions. It is used by accounts payable to verify appropriate signature authorizations for invoice payment. It is also linked to our Lotus Notes expense account system for routing of the expense accounts to the appropriate approver. A purchasing rep is responsible for updating the approver database. Updates are simple to do and are effective immediately.

- Manual signatures are verified to imaged authorization signatures. The online images can be accessed via the Microsoft Imager (which comes with Windows 95). Imaged signatures are stored by last name, first name, and middle initial. Each signature is a separate form that can be accessed from Microsoft Explorer. By double-clicking on the appropriate name, the image is displayed.

Either of these techniques, or a variation thereof, can be used by accounts payable professionals interested in updating signature verification procedures. Whether one of these is used or not, an important part of any accounts payable procedures should include the updating of an approval listing along with some sort of record of the signatures of all approvers. While these techniques are not guaranteed to thwart an employee intent on committing fraud, they will make a serious dent in the process. They will also prevent others from either intentionally or unintentionally overstepping their approval levels.

2.2B PROPER CHECK-SIGNING PROCEDURES AND CONTROL (NEW)

"Trust is not an internal control," says Margolin, Winer & Evens, a Garden City, New York, accounting firm, in its semimonthly publication, *Fraud Alert*. Many companies with excellent controls become lax when it comes to their check-signing procedures, often because of the involvement of upper management. Many sign whatever is "put under their nose" making them perfect targets for employees intent on committing internal check fraud.

(a) Best Practice for Check Signing

When checks are given for signature, they should be accompanied by enough paperwork so that the signer can verify that the check has been made out properly and for the correct amount. At a minimum, this should include the purchase order (PO) completely filled out, the receiving report, and the original invoice. The invoice should indicate that someone has checked the price and quantity extensions on the invoice. It adds that the signer should randomly double-check the math on the invoice.

This may seem like a lot of work, but remember, it is not for all checks. It is only for those that are to be manually signed, which are those over a set dollar amount and represent the largest exposure for the company. It is also recommended that any discrepancies on the three-way match be noted.

The *Fraud Alert* also suggests that:

- Particular care be taken with vendors with unusual names and addresses.
- The check payee should match the invoice information.
- No abbreviations should be used on checks. It is relatively simple for ABC to be altered to read A. B. Callahan.

(b) Limits

Many companies put manual signatures only on checks over a certain dollar amount. Others require two signatures on checks over an even higher dollar amount. Given the amount of money involved and the damage that a fraudulent loss can do to the underpinnings of a company, having two manual signatures on very large checks is not a bad idea.

Proper check-signing procedures do not end once the ink dries on the check. The checks need to be returned to someone other than the requestor and separate from the record-keeping function. An independent party should mail the checks.

A few companies require that all travel and entertainment (T&E) reports be manually signed. The reason for this is that many believe that employees, knowing a high-level executive will be looking at their expense reports, tend to put the brakes on their spending when on company business.

These procedures may make it seem like overkill. However, given the high incidence of fraudulent disbursements, a little extra care is well worth the effort. While good up-front controls are one of the first lines of defense against disbursement fraud, good check-signing procedures can catch those last-minute frauds that managed to slip through the first go-round.

p. 30. Insert at end of chapter:

2.7 CANCELLED CHECKS AND IRATE VENDORS (NEW)

Most accounts payable professionals can list their "worst" vendors from memory. Suppliers make this list prepared by the A/P staff. One frustrated accounts payable manager recently vented on the accounts payable discussion group as follows:

> We deal with around 25,000 vendors and send out approximately 3,000 checks per week. We get a tremendous number of vendors who post our checks wrong. Even when we have more than one invoice on the same check (especially phone companies), they will show one invoice paid but not all. They insist the only way to clear their error is to receive a copy of the cancelled check. This is most aggravating because I feel like I am doing their job as well as my own. We list all the information they need on the check stub. Every time they tell us we owe an invoice, we show that invoice paid. They think we should pay what they say, or figure it out for them. I get so mad. Unbelievable . . . and I thought we were the customer!

This posting touched a nerve in the accounts payable community. Here are some of the suggestions offered by other accounts payable professionals who have experienced similar problems:

> **Get everyone together.** "We have encountered a similar situation with a vendor who is our main source of office

supplies," says another accounts payable manager. "After numerous attempts to work with the vendor's accounts receivable department without success, I arranged a meeting with our purchasing manager to request we find another supplier. Before taking that step, we set up a joint meeting with the vendor." (The purchasing manager was in agreement with my position, and agreed to pull the account if the vendor was unwilling to take the necessary steps to correct the situation.) The meeting included the sales rep, the accounts receivable rep, and the ordering rep.

"Once the sales rep realized that we were on the verge of pulling the account, he made arrangements to have one person handle our account. The company also agreed to preaudit all invoices prior to delivery to accounts payable. We send our checks to the contact person who ensures that payments are credited correctly. This has eliminated hours of recreating information that has already been provided to the vendor, along with eliminating 95% of the billing errors we were spending time researching and correcting."

This person was extremely lucky in that the purchasing professional agreed to support accounts payable. This factor, along with support from senior management, can be crucial in getting a key vendor to change its wayward ways.

Charge them for the service. "I agree with what the other post has to say about this subject," says still another accounts payable professional who has spent more than a few hours doing another company's work. "In our case, we've had this happen a few times and tried to deal with the credit clerk to clear up the problem. When it became clear that we were doing their work, we decided to play hardball. First, we charged them $10 for every check copy they requested from our own files, or those ordered from the bank. We imposed this on vendors who had a track record of requesting copies of checks. Believe it or not, this seemed to really clear up the problem with most problem vendors." This is an excellent suggestion as it is unlikely that the clerks on the other side are going to want to explain the bill for such services to their management.

Go right to the top. Another manager stepped up to the plate to recount another tale of rogue vendors. "Unfortunately, there were tougher vendors who really just didn't get it," says this pro. "They constantly rebilled us under various names, didn't record our payments properly, etc. I finally made the decision to call the president of the company and deal with this.

"Of course, most of the time, you can only get through to their assistant, but they seem to almost always get results. Don't be too sweet either . . . always be professional, but firm. Demonstrate, through your tone and words, that you are frustrated and expect results. Tell them everything that has happened. (You should be keeping notes on problem vendors.) Tell them who you talked to, what was said, and how long you've been dealing with the problem. If the head of the organization can't fix it, maybe it's time to switch vendors."

Before following this first-rate advice, make sure your management is okay with this approach. Some will not be. True, often it is difficult to get through to a high-level executive, as most have secretaries screening their calls. If you encounter such resistance, try calling before 8:30 in the morning when most high senior executives are at their desks and their secretaries have not arrived. You might be surprised to discover who you can get on the phone at that hour.

Take them off the approved vendor list. The last resort is to *disapprove* a vendor. To do this, you will need the concurrence of your procurement department. "Simply tell the vendor (call the president for this, too!) that you want to close your account," says the accounts payable professional recommending this technique. "Tell them they are not permitted to accept any further orders from you. If they think they will lose your business, they will act quickly to resolve the issues. If all else fails, maybe it is time to really remove them from your approved vendor database," she concludes.

One check per invoice. If your accounting system supports this feature, one solution is to instruct the system at the vendor level to not combine several invoices on one payment, advises another manager. "We routinely use this feature whenever we have problem vendors or vendors whose invoices do not have invoice numbers. Many banks also support online printing of cancelled checks (front and back), which can be a big time-saver," she adds.

Multipronged approach. "I think the time has come to play hardball," says the final advisor. She recommends the following multistep process:

1. Escalate the issue to the most senior finance person you can who will have the clout to do something; if need be, take it to the chief financial officer/chief executive officer. (If you have a sales rep, you can obtain names and titles from them; also let the sales rep know how serious you are so he or she can notify management.)

2. If feasible, tell the vendor you are not issuing any more payments until the account is cleared. This should stop them from taking new orders. Obviously, notify the district offices of this action and the reasons behind it. If any employees want to use the vendor, tell them to put it on a corporate procurement card (p-card) or pay it themselves and expense-report it, but no direct billing.

3. Obtain a report from your system of all payments issued to the vendor containing invoice and check numbers and send it to the person with clout (step 1). Also, forward this to their finance department with instructions to reconcile the account.

Those accounts payable managers who have encountered problems of this nature may find some relief in the recommendations from their peers in the trenches. The strategies suggested above have worked for them and may very well work for you.

3

Exception and
Rush Processing

p. 36. Insert after first full paragraph:

3.3A   MODIFY SYSTEMS AND PROCEDURES TO REDUCE THE NEED FOR RUSH CHECKS (NEW)

Sometimes the reason companies have so many "rush" checks is that their policies and procedures have not been updated for a long time. In a recent survey of subscribers by the Institute of Management and Administration's (IOMA's) report on *Managing Accounts Payable,* a surprising number of participants indicated that they had been able to not only reduce the number of exception checks, but make their departments more efficient simply by revising their policies and procedures. The respondents shared their strategies for accomplishing this amazing feat. We reviewed these innovative suggestions and compiled the best of them here.

Although many of the comments were similar, most showed how accounts payable professionals with limited resources or constrained by corporate circumstances manage to run a productive department. A review of the comments also demonstrates that accounts payable has moved to center stage in corporate financial management.

(a) Trends

Here are some of the changes mentioned by numerous respondents:

- A growing number of companies have formalized accounts payable procedures documented in a company-wide procedures manual.

- Benchmarking is becoming more commonplace not only to measure departmental productivity, but also to identify business problems.

- Accounts payable professionals are not tolerating the additional work related to *rush* checks when it is caused repeatedly by the careless actions of others outside the department.

- Accounts payable professionals are learning how to use common software (e.g., Excel, Lotus, Word) and are using this knowledge to develop procedures that greatly improve the departmental efficiency.

- Accounts payable departments are insisting that the purchasing department correctly and completely fill out purchase orders (POs). A large number are refusing to do the clean-up work for the purchasing department.

(b) A Whole New World

The positive tone of the responses along with the high professionalism of the responses indicates that the accounts payable world across much of corporate America is changing. Those looking to improve their own departmental productivity can review the responses of their peers to find what will work in their own companies. By emulating the success of others, accounts payable professionals can put themselves in the best position to find process improvements that will work. Remember the procedures that have been in place the longest are the ones that should be evaluated most closely. The odds are high that that is where the biggest productivity gains can be found.

(c) Best Strategies

- Produce an accounts payable policy and procedure manual to be used by the entire company. Whenever a PO, check request, expense report, or other item is submitted incorrectly, photocopy the appropriate page from the manual and return it along with the incorrectly filled-out form to the submitter.

- Take courses to learn how to use software such as Access, Excel, Word, and the like. Use the new knowledge to design management and departmental reports.

- Develop a set of procedures to handle invoices from the receipt of the bill until the final payment goes out the door.

- Take advantage of the changeover to reevaluate and streamline current procedures when putting in a new computer system.

- Increase the limit for petty cash reimbursements to a reasonable level. This reduces the number of reimbursements needed. If possible, get rid of the petty cash function completely.

- Require everyone to follow set procedures. Do not make exceptions for favorites or friends.

- Move the check-printing process from a dot matrix printer to a laser printer. Not only will the checks have a more professional look, they will also take less time to run.

- Develop standard forms for use within the accounts payable department and by those requesting information or checks from accounts payable.

- Set up a vendor master for intercompany vendors so that invoices entered for those vendors will automatically pick up the correct general ledger coding.

- Consolidate billings from frequent vendors. Multiple weekly invoices can be paid from one monthly statement on the 15th of the following month.

- Set base terms at FOB your city for freight term clarification. Create a label with your phone number and place it on the check stub when not paying the freight charged by the vendor.

- Improve the review and approval process, and have reviewers take ownership of what they approve. This will reduce mistakes and the number of duplicate payments.

- Implement account rules to catch system errors.

- Learn as much as possible about different accounting systems. After your company gets ready to move to a new system, you will be able to provide input as to which software offers the best accounts payable functions.

- Promote efficiencies and limit invoice handling using the 80/20 rule and materiality limits. Focus attention on higher-dollar purchases, not the small-dollar items.

- Realign departmental duties to make the workload more evenly distributed and the department more efficient.

- Implement a system that will permit online research of the three-way match and payment problems. This can eliminate many phone calls and save much time formerly spent on manual research.

- Although promoting from within has many advantages, occasionally it is not the best option. When the opportunity presents itself, hire a new set of eyes from outside the department and/or company to review policies and procedures.

- After publishing a corporate policy and procedures manual, measure and report findings to reduce exception items and costs.

- Centralize accounts payable operations, eliminating duplication of efforts.

- Provide adequate technology training for the entire accounts payable department, not just the manager.

- Review batch invoices against batch edit reports and make all deletions and/or changes before cutting checks. This will reduce the number of checks that need to be voided after the run.

- File invoices by batch rather than vendor. With a decent tracking system, you will be able to identify which batch a particular invoice is associated with should it need to be pulled at a later date.

- Rewrite programs to ease the payment process of airfare invoices.

- Simplify controls without adding risk.

- Insist that POs be filled out completely and accurately or return them to the person submitting them.

- Use measurement tools to monitor accounts payable activities. Analyze this information to determine the root cause for discrepancies. Once the causes have been identified, create procedures to eliminate them.

- Make the purchasing agents responsible for their vendor relations, purchases, costs, general ledger accounts, and discounts. Have the purchaser supply all pertinent information on the PO, or make it their responsibility to come into the accounting department to correct any problems, missing information, or discrepancies.

- Encourage the use of p-cards and corporate travel cards throughout the company so that invoices for certain items never come to the accounts payable department.

- Improve communications with other departments by reviewing procedures and streamlining them so the new measures work for both departments.

- Push back the resolution of discrepancy issues to purchasing. This forces the party with the most information (and often the one that caused the problem in the first place) to resolve the problem.

- Stop filing check copies (or check stubs) by vendor or with invoices. File the copies separately by batch, or move to a check form that does not produce copies.

- Review procedures that have been in effect for years. The odds are great that some of the new technologies, such as p-cards, new methods of travel and entertainment (T&E) reimbursements, and so on, are not being utilized.

- Use benchmarking to pinpoint problem areas. These can include identifying departments that have invoices sent to them instead of accounts payable, those departments not completing POs, and those who constantly request rush checks because invoices get lost on their desks.

- Review the check-printing timing. Can the number of check runs be decreased without increasing the number of requests for *rush* checks? Or, perhaps, should the number of runs be increased to eliminate a large number of requests for rush checks?

- Track invoices sent out for approval on computer. Produce a report several times a week to identify bottlenecks. With the hard evidence in hand, discuss the issues with the appropriate personnel and eliminate the problems.

- Hold meetings with other department heads to find ways to improve interactions between departments, standardize procedures, and enhance the image of the accounts payable department throughout the company.

By employing the techniques discussed above, accounts payable professionals will not only make a dent in the number of "rush" checks requested, they will improve the overall efficiency of the department.

4

Errors and
Duplicate Payments

p. 43. Insert at end of page:

4.5A SETTING UP A DO-IT-YOURSELF AUDIT THAT CUTS DUPLICATE PAYMENTS (NEW)

Do you really need an internal accounts payable audit team? "Yes," says Wendy Visger, Nordstrom's accounts payable systems assistant manager. The chief benefit of the do-it-yourself approach is that your firm keeps 100% of what it finds. Following are some of Visger's secrets for making in-house audits work.

(a) Why Self-Audit?

In addition to retaining all the savings, an in-house audit team can provide training and make recommendations to the company immediately; thus, needed changes are made to plug the holes through which recoverable funds leak. Visger says that the ability to locate and identify necessary policy and system changes immediately can save money another way. By finding the duplicate payments before they go, the company saves the time and effort invested to recover the funds after the fact.

(b) Training an In-House A/P Audit Team

Learn from outside auditors. After all, they are the professionals. Ideally, they visit not only your company but also others in the same industry. The accounts payable manager responsible for the audit group should see where the outside auditors are placing their focus and learn new trends in auditing from them. Get written directions from outside audit firms when doing an in-house audit.
Additionally:

- Hire auditors who have come up through the ranks in the accounts payable department.
- Pair new auditors with experienced hands.
- Invest in training, specifically phone skills, personal computer skills, and negotiating skills.
- Have auditors do audit work only. They should not be doing regular accounts payable tasks as well.
- Give experienced auditors the authority to cancel claims and negotiate settlements as needed.

(c) Designing Reports

Auditors not only need reports to work from, they need to prepare reports to identify weaknesses in existing policies and procedures. To design the most effective reports, ask the following questions:

- What are you finding in the audit?
- How can you get a report to provide the needed information?
- What do you want the report to accomplish?
- What fields are needed?

Once the answers to these questions are obtained, it is possible to design the reports. The following tips will make it easier:

- Place the fields so the report is easy to work with.

- Have the report do as much of the work as possible. It can summarize, sort, subtotal, calculate discounts and percentages, and flag items such as new categories to the report or new fields entered by outside auditors.

If the data must be sorted in different ways or manipulated, make it possible to download the data to Excel or Access.

(d)   Types of Reports

(i) Expense. When most people think about accounts payable audits, they focus on duplicate payments. To uncover such payments, arrange the information by preparing reports to show:

- Same vendor number, same cost, cost exceeds $50.00
- Same vendor number, same document number, different cost
- Same document number and cost, different vendor number
- All duplicate payments by descending dollar amount

(ii) Merchandise. Use five different exception reports for merchandise:

- *Vendor historical.* This report shows the entire history for each vendor. It recovers discount dollars, locates errors made in accounts payable, and demonstrates vendor trends.
- *Claim reporting.* If the company needs an indication of mark-up percentages that are out of the norm and claims that are processed for the wrong amounts, a claim report would be appropriate.
- *Discount by PO.* To find discounts not taken when the invoices were paid, prepare this report.
- *Purchase Order Notes.* This report captures free-form notes entered by buyers on POs. This can result in freight and special-deal dollars being recovered.

- *Sales Reports.* To show style price and terms comparisons for special-event POs, prepare this report.

(e) Using Statements

Some vendors are notorious about hiding credits from their customers. Consequently, some accounts payable professionals periodically call their largest vendors and ask for statements—not to make payments but to uncover such credits. When asking for these statements, it is important that the accounts payable manager stipulate that the statement show not only outstanding amounts but all credits as well. Some tricky credit managers will send along statements without the necessary credit information.

The following three points show how to handle statements and credit memos:

1. Send letters to all vendors that meet a set dollar criterion on a biennial basis.
2. Work the statements to locate credits indicating dollars due to the company.
3. Call vendors to verify large-dollar credits before taking deductions.

The last step is important, as it prevents problems down the road.

(f) Additional Tips

To help reduce duplicate payments further:

- Communicate with the merchants who hold the key to special agreements.
- Educate the rest of the company as to what a post audit is.
- Publish and promote the results of the audit and what it has added to the bottom line.
- Make recommendations for changes where errors are discovered.

- Follow up to make sure safeguards are put in place.
- Follow a stringent schedule of auditing all processes on a rotating basis.
- Make system changes wherever possible to reduce the work coming to the audit team and have the deduction taken at the time of initial payment to the vendor.

(g)   Timing

At a recent conference, an accounts payable auditor confided that one of her clients had her firm come in only once every three years. Though such timing has the advantage of minimal disruption, it has a number of downsides, too, including:

- *Unhappy vendors.* Credit managers do not really like getting hit by postaudit claims. It makes additional work for them. The further back in time the items are, the harder it is for them to find the necessary backup. Asking them to pay back money that is three years old infuriates them. Although no vendor likes to research a payment, the sooner it is presented, the less disruption it is likely to cause. Visger has merchandise audits performed biennially covering a six-month period that is never more than one year prior. Expense audits are performed annually covering one year at a time. This lessens vendor correspondence and disputes.
- *Higher claims.* One of the benefits of having an outside audit is to identify the weak spots in your policies, systems, and procedures. By having the audits performed more frequently, it is possible to limit the amounts paid to outside auditors.

p. 50. Insert after carryover paragraph:

4.10A ELIMINATING DUPLICATE PAYMENTS WITHOUT AN AUDITOR (NEW)

Duplicate payments are a serious issue for most companies. In fact, in the latest *IOMA Benchmarking Survey*, 90% of the respondents admitted making one or more duplicate payments in the last year. At the recent IOMA/IMI Accounts Payable conference, Beverly Brando Gillilian, of Business Strategies Inc. in Michigan, showed accounts payable pros how to find these errors. She also revealed how to get management to change the procedures that allowed for duplicate payments.

(a) Duplicate Payments—Phase One

Most accounts payable professionals know which problem customers are likely to receive duplicate payments. Gillilian suggests that you prepare a list of such vendors and then ask your information technology department to run three reports by vendor. These reports should show payments made to each vendor by:

- Invoice number
- Dollar amount
- Invoice date

Group this information together by vendor and review again to further identify duplicates. This step alone may provide the accounts payable manager with the data needed to finally get the master vendor file cleaned up.

A manual review of these reports will identify those payments that must be further investigated. While this research is being done, collect all backup information as to why the duplicate payment was made.

The recovery work should not begin without approval from the accounts payable manager's supervisor. It is crucial that this issue be handled appropriately as it offers an excellent chance for accounts payable professionals to improve their stock with upper management and tighten procedures. Gillilian advises turning this potential bomb into a great opportunity.

(b)   Handling the Criticism

After gathering the backup information for each duplicate payment, avoid placing blame. Rather, search for the operational "weak links" that cause the majority of the problems. Rush checks, for example, are often at the root of duplicate payments.

Identify these weak links and include them in a report to management. "Not only will this information protect the accounts payable department," says Gillilian, "but it gives the accounts payable manager the ammunition needed to force change." When there is documentation showing that the company made $2 million in duplicate payments because of rush checks, management will pay attention.

There is another financial advantage in having the accounts payable professional handle the duplicate payments as described above. Third-party audit firms typically charge a percentage that can run as high as 50%. Thus, a company with $2 million in duplicate payments could pay the outside firm as much as $1 million to recover the funds. If you do the job, the cost to your company is much lower. Even if one or two people have to be added to the staff to handle the work, your firm will still be ahead of the game financially.

It is highly recommended that management approval be obtained before chasing suppliers for the return of funds. Sometimes management may only decide to make sure the duplicate payments do not happen again. This can happen if one of the suppliers is also on the company's board of directors.

(c)   The Second Phase

Once the first cut has been thoroughly analyzed, it is time for the next step. Although many accounts payable managers believe they know to whom the duplicate payments are going, they may not be correct. Therefore, it is recommended that the process be conducted for all large and possibly even mid-sized vendors. There may be additional revenues to be had from these sources.

(d) The Third Phase

Many companies do a very poor job of cleaning up their master vendor files. The same company could be in there several times under slightly different names. This is one of the leading causes of duplicate payments. First, request a list of all the vendors in the master vendor file. Then, review the list carefully to determine which vendors are actually duplicates.

By quantifying the losses due to duplicate payments, one will be armed with the information needed to change those procedures that cause problems. Best of all, the company will be able to recover 100% of the duplicate payments for itself.

With a little effort, it is possible to uncover duplicate payments yourself without having to pay a third party to find them for you.

4.10B BATCH DATA ENTRY (NEW)

One of the best ways to catch errors early on is to create a batch when entering information. Many accounts payable departments use this method to detect human errors made when entering data. This method is used in over three-quarters of all companies with neither company size nor industry having a serious impact on its usage. See Exhibit 4.1 for a breakdown of the information.

Exhibit 4.1   **When You Create a Batch, Do You Have Immediate (Daily) Error Detection?**

	Yes	*No*
	78.4%	21.6%
By Size of Company	*Yes (%)*	*No (%)*
Up to 99	76.4	23.6
100–249	74.2	25.8
250–499	73.7	26.3
500–999	82.4	17.6
1,000–4,999	76.4	23.6
Over 5,000	83.6	16.4
By Industry		
Manufacturing	78.1	21.9
Finance	85.7	14.3
Utilities, transportation	77.6	22.4
Private practice	75.5	24.5
Nonprofit	73.0	27.0
Wholesale/retail/distribution	78.3	21.7
Health care	76.8	23.2
Education	84.0	16.0
Media	80.6	19.4
Construction	86.4	13.6
Entertainment/hospitality	66.7	33.3
Other	78.8	21.2

Source: IOMA.

* 4.10C DUPLICATE PAY AUDITS: THE FUTURE OF ACCOUNTS PAYABLE AND A/P AUDITS (NEW)

A revolution is underway in accounts payable. Even organizations that were considered leading edge a few short years ago would today be viewed as backward. The changes are occurring rapidly and have only just begun. A panel discussion of seven experts at IOMA's Accounts Payable Conference and Expo in October 2002 explored the issues and provided a glimpse into what is to come. The group, led by Process Management Improvement's Tom Nichols, surveyed the profession, its use of audit firms, and where audit firms will fit in the grand scheme in a few years. From these discussions, coupled with the insightful questions from the audience, came a surprising but energizing picture of the accounts payable world in the next decade.

(a) Trends

The conference session began with each panelist briefly stating his or her views on where the accounts payable profession was going, the future of the audit industry, and how he or she fit in. A few notable trends emerged from the comments. They are:

- Contract management and compliance is the next hot area for audits. Expect to hear a lot about the losses due not to duplicate pays but to lack of contract compliance. To put the issue into some perspective, one of the speakers indicated that, on average, a company using an audit saves:
    - 1 percent of spend on accounts payable audits
    - 3 to 8 percent of spend on contract compliance errors
- Accounts payable and purchasing departments will continue to merge.
- Accounts payable organizations will become less transaction-oriented and more analytical. This trend will be magnified as companies move toward electronic invoicing.

- Technology will play a big part in both accounts payable operations and the way firms audit for all sorts of erroneous payments.
- In even greater numbers, companies will recover the low-hanging erroneous payment fruit themselves. They will do this by using technology, using some of the features of their ERP systems, plugging the holes that caused the problems in the first place, and by doing their own internal audits.

(b)   Compensation

One of the issues frequently raised when discussing audit firms is the matter of how the auditors' staffs are compensated. Before discussing the merits and shortcomings of each, it's important to look at the two underlying philosophies under which most audit firms work. The first, which most will readily own up to, is that the firm wants to do a good job for its clients so it will be invited back the following year for a repeat engagement.

The second philosophy is in direct opposition to the first. One audit firm, for example, indicated that its goal is *not* to be invited back the following year. Jarring as this may sound, the firm has a good explanation. This firm focuses on identifying the holes that allow erroneous payments and then helping companies that have these gaps to fill them. The firm's philosophy is that if it is successful the first time, there will be little or nothing for it to collect on its clients' behalf the second time around.

The compensation schemes in use include:

- Auditors on a fixed salary
- Auditors who are compensated (or incited) through a commission structure
- Auditors who are paid a base salary and a percentage of corporate profits (or participate in a bonus pool based on whether the firm as a whole meets or exceeds its revenue targets)

The fixed-salary proponents point out that they are willing to go after all erroneous payments, not just the large-dollar ones; in contrast, the commission people assert that they are not tempted to stay at an engagement one day longer than necessary. The real decision, then, is perhaps that the compensation structure doesn't matter as much as the level of the recoveries.

(c)   Measuring the Success of the Audit Firm

There is a relatively easy way to determine whether the firm you hired did a good job or not. Hire a second firm to do a second pass and see how much its auditors collect. Many charge a higher fee for this type of work because the first firm will have made all the easy recoveries. This is quite common, and the audit firms not only expect it, they encourage it. If you are taking this approach, bid the work out. Since many in the business know each other and the others' work so well, they will often bid lower if they know who did the primary audit.

The bidding process can work both ways. One firm confided that it never bid to go in after a certain competitor—because it never found anything. This led the auditor to conclude that the two firms must use similar audit techniques. Don't be shy about asking for a reaudit—it's done all the time.

Also common are the audits of outsourced work, especially companies handling telecommunication, utility, and freight payments. The speakers at the IOMA conference felt that audits of payments made by third-party vendors were critical.

(d)   Working with Purchasing

The best audits are those that cover the entire procure-to-pay cycle. This requires cooperation between the two departments, which is often difficult to get if the two groups don't have the same manager. Several attendees indicated that they had a hard time getting purchasing to agree to audits. The speakers had several suggestions on how to get cooperation. They included:

- Allocate the recoveries back to purchasing through an accounting entry.

- Find a "smoking gun" to convince them of the value of an audit. The smoking gun could be a returned check from a vendor or a credit on a statement. Whenever you find a credit on a statement, investigate the root cause of the credit. It may uncover one of those communication gaps that permit other flawed payments.

- Provide purchasing with reports showing spend analysis, price spikes, and case studies where a contract was in a drawer and invoicing was done against a blanket PO that was missing key terms.

Once purchasing is shown several cases where the supplier has overbilled, and payment was made at the higher price because the necessary information was not put on the PO, they will be more likely to cooperate. Also, as companies continue to look for new ways to save money, contract compliance audits will become more common.

(e)   Working on Your Own

One of the attendees at the conference asked what an accounts payable professional should look for if purchasing was not cooperating with even the idea of an audit. The speakers suggested:

- Discounted vendors
- Missed rebate opportunities
- Complex pricing arrangements—a definite red flag that the pricing might be prone to errors

The accounts payable professional working without purchasing should also focus on the vendor file setup, from the beginning of the relationship. By setting firm rules on how the vendor invoices, the format of these invoices, and the frequency of the invoices, some of the problems may be eliminated. The move to Web invoicing will also have a positive impact on the problem of incorrect payments.

(f) The Experts Speak Out on the Future of A/P and A/P Audits

To stay ahead of the curve, accounts payable professionals need to get ready for the future. The views of the professionals shared at this forum provide some guideposts for those looking to continue in the game.

(i) American Express—Dan Whelan

Accounts payable organizations will need to be more efficient and effective. The main tool to accomplish this is automation. As accounts payable departments become more successful, there will be a reduction in recoveries. Therefore, the accounts payable audit firms must add specialized services to their repertoire. Some of these value-added services might include:

- Enhanced reporting
- Improved communication with internal audit in identifying the root causes and elimination of duplicate pays
- Spend management and the formation of strategic alliances to offer broader range of services

(ii) Apex Analytix—Jim Arnold

There will be a convergence of accounts payable and purchasing. The accounts payable team will become less transaction-oriented and more strategic in focus. Organizations are becoming metrics-driven: "If you can't measure it, you can't manage it."

Real-time audits, using technology, is rapidly becoming the ultimate objective. While it is nice to recover money in an audit, an even better tactic is to not have the money go out the door in the first place. Companies will proactively manage their audits.

(iii) Business Strategies—Dan Geelhoed

The duplicate payment side of the auditing business is giving way to technology. The audit industry is changing at light speed. Accounts payable and purchasing are merging in many organizations. The recovery firm that will be successful in the future is the one that focuses on nontraditional areas such as:

- Telecom
- Utilities
- Freight
- Sales and use tax

(iv) Connolly Consulting Assoc.—Larry Connolly

The root cause of duplicate payments hasn't changed. Complexity in a production environment with constraints on resources remains the key driver of mistakes. It is an industry that had $2.5 billion in recoveries in 2001. The future will be in contract compliance reviews where there are more recovery opportunities. The IT challenges remain, with data sets getting bigger.

Capturing price concessions contained in e-mails, not documents, will be a real challenge. Companies will benefit from competition among audit firms because:

- Low-hanging fruit will go away as software and more efficient outsourcing find their way into the corporate arena.
- There will be more "Pepsi challenges" as companies adopt policies against sole sources and require the flip-flopping of audit firms every year. Reaudits will also play a key role.
- The demand for value-added services is growing.

(v) PRG Shultz—Andrew Schlegel

Accounts payable professionals drive the trends in the industry. It's all about efficiency, which translates into reducing both the number of transactions and people. The challenge that faces the audit firms as the paper trails disappear is technology-driven.

The future for the audit firms is in auditing the entire procure-to-pay cycle and providing value-added reports to customers.

(vi) Recap—Jon Casher

The role of accounts payable and accounts payable recovery is changing, and dramatically. In many organizations, accounts payable and purchasing will merge. It has already happened in many service organizations. There will be fewer people in accounts payable, but visibility will increase.

Accounts payable will do virtually no data entry as invoices and expense reports are received electronically. The accounts payable professional will focus on quality assurance and contract and policy compliance. Accounts payable will also be responsible for more reporting and analysis.

Accounts payable recovery firms have been, and will continue to become, partners with their clients. They will focus more on value-added consulting services and helping their clients catch most erroneous payments and billing errors. Contract compliance and specialized audits that require knowledge of vendor billing practices will be the main sources of recoveries by these firms.

(vii) Stout Causey & Horning—Tom Stout

Accounts payable organizations will look for strategic partners not only to recover erroneous payments but also to decrease the cost of providing services to internal clients. The pressure to keep headcount to a minimum in many organizations has caused some money to fall through the cracks. The main cause for this is due to the communication gaps between accounts payable and procurement and accounts payable and shipping and receiving. The effective audit firm will look at those gaps and provide root cause analysis, along with training, to eliminate the errors that are under their control.

The firm will also work with purchasing to provide tools to eliminate problems before the checks are written. The successful audit firm of the future will help its clients analyze their total spend.

5

Paying When the Original Invoice Is Not Available

5.1 WHO PAYS FROM COPIES

p. 52. Delete Exhibit 5.1 and replace with the following:

Exhibit 5.1 **Who Pays from Copies?**

	Yes	No
	53.2%	46.8%
By Size of Company	Yes (%)	No (%)
Up to 99	53.6	46.4
100–249	51.6	48.4
250–499	48.2	51.8
500–999	47.6	52.4
1,000–4,999	53.0	47.0
Over 5,000	62.7	37.3
By Industry		
Manufacturing	55.7	44.3
Finance	57.4	42.6
Utilities/transportation	42.9	57.1
Private practice	57.7	42.3
Nonprofit/government	46.2	53.8
Wholesale/retail/distribution	51.9	48.1
Health care	40.6	59.4
Education	68.0	32.0
Communications	46.9	53.1
Construction	54.5	45.5
Entertainment/hospitality	55.6	44.4
Other	58.8	41.2

Source: IOMA.

Part Two

The People

6

Making Your Accounts Payable Department First Rate

p. 63. Insert after carryover list:

6.2A HIRING (NEW)

Given the hot job market, hiring good entry-level staff has turned into a nightmare for many accounts payable managers. Once hired, retaining competent staff is no picnic either. In fact, at the IOMA/IMI Accounts Payable conference, Robert Half International's Carrie Buchwald said that the most challenging position for her search firm to fill is that of the accounts payable professional. She went on to share proven hiring and motivating strategies.

(a) What Does Not Work

"Don't use blind advertisements," warns Buchwald. Candidates will not respond for fear that their résumés will end up on their bosses' desks. Given the shift in the hiring climate, employers must now sell their companies to prospective employees. She recommends emphasizing all the positive aspects of the corporate culture of your company so interviewees will want to work in your department.

(b) Effective Hiring Strategies

Many accounts payable managers would like to hire college graduates. Unfortunately, the salaries offered by most companies for their entry-level accounts payable positions cannot compete with those given for other accounting positions. Thus, those doing the hiring have to be creative if they wish to get competent staff. Here are some techniques that work:

- *Set up a training program for administrative people.* Many companies have very competent administrative assistants who have no upward mobility. They would love to work in accounts payable but lack the basic skills needed. Give these hard workers the opportunity to learn and grow with your accounts payable department and you will have a loyal employee for a long time.

- *Begin recruiting at colleges for temporary positions.* Doing so, especially at Christmas and during the summer, will give you some exposure to potential employees and give them a taste of accounts payable.

- *Set up a formal mentoring program.* Assign more experienced staff to work with newcomers. This might work well in conjunction with the first recommendation above. Not only does mentoring ensure that the new employee get off on the right foot, it serves as a positive motivational tool for the employee doing the mentoring. It shows they are trusted and valued.

- *Ongoing training is important for both new and old employees.* Technology will continue to play a key role in process improvements in accounts payable. By providing the necessary training to the staff, their motivation will be high and they will not feel like they must leave in order to keep their skills current. Excel, Internet, Word, and basic accounting are a few of the areas where training can be offered to the entire staff relatively easily.

- *Consider hiring graduates from two-year colleges.* This approach works particularly well at those companies that offer tuition reimbursement to employees continuing their education. By the time employees have completed their four-year degrees, their salaries will have gone up through raises to a point where it is competitive with other departments.

(c)   Hidden Costs of New Hires

Some people do not realize how costly turnover can be. In addition to the costs of hiring (advertisements, agency fees, temporary help salaries, etc.), there are the costs that do not show up. There may be additional overtime needed not only to train the new person but to get the daily work completed while the new employee gets up to speed. Additionally, new employees and temporaries are likely to make mistakes during the training process. It takes time to correct these errors, and that is costly as well.

Given the costs and aggravation of hiring new staff, many seasoned executives have come to the conclusion that it is a better strategy to take care of the existing staff than to have to hire a new one. Accounts payable professionals who motivate their existing staff using some of Buchwald's advice are less likely to need her first-rate hiring strategies.

7

Managing the Staff (New)

p. 86. Insert new section:

7.6   MANAGING A UNIONIZED STAFF (NEW)

Working with a union staff in accounts payable can present some unique challenges. It also draws attention to several crucial management issues that can benefit all A/P managers—including staff motivation, negotiation and compromise, and staff communications. "For us here at Southern California Gas Company," says Tom Solum, accounts payable manager, "working with a union has been a positive experience." We spoke to several accounts payable professionals, including Solum and Tom Nichols, a principal in an accounts payable consulting firm, to gather their views about working with unions in general, as well as specific issues around the use of technology, motivation, and special accommodations.

While running AT&T's accounts payable operations, Nichols managed two locations that consolidated the accounts payable operations for the company. He says that since both Florida and Georgia, where the operations were located, were "right-to-work" states, union membership was not a condition of employment. Nevertheless, with union members making up an estimated one-third of the employees in his departments, he still had to abide by union guidelines. Like the many others who are constrained by union rules, he has found ways to turn working with unions to his advantage.

Solum explains: "Management/union rights, relationships, and responsibilities are spelled out in a negotiated agreement between the company and the union with respect to rates of pay and other conditions of employment. There are formal grievance procedures to follow if the parties cannot settle disputes at the local level."

(a) Compromise Is the Answer

The relationship between management and employees is fragile. The work environment, as Solum explains, can run the gamut from a great place to work to one in which everyone is using the current job as just a stepping stone to interview for other opportunities. Establishing clear expectations and consistently treating employees with respect can go a long way toward creating a good work environment. Drawing on his experience, Solum argues that proposed changes to work practices need to be discussed and agreed upon between management and employees. In that way, by the time the decision becomes final, most employees will have already bought into the change.

Nichols has mixed thoughts on the question. "In times of economic prosperity and stability," he says, "where cost and competitive pressures are few, there are minimal problems in managing a unionized organization. In a tighter economy, it can be difficult to manage given that both parties have their own agendas. The decision by management to play hardball, however, could result in arbitration and mediation becoming a way of life. Such an environment becomes costly, and people lose focus on their primary goal of satisfying customer needs. The only short-term approach is to recognize where differences exist and attempt to find a compromise."

(b) Benefits

There are some very real advantages associated with working with a union staff—benefits that are often overlooked. "The union leadership is uniquely positioned to provide information and perspectives about an organization's systems and employee attitudes," says Nichols. "They can challenge company policies that they believe are nonproductive, and provide support and encouragement to their members in an ever-changing accounts payable environment."

And that's not all. "We have a very low turnover," notes Solum. "When we do have an opening," he says, "the job is posted and filled by those qualified applicants with the most seniority. This means that most new employees to the group are already highly knowledgeable about the company. Rules for vacation scheduling, who gets overtime, work shortages, and layoffs are well defined and follow established procedures. Performance expectations are clearly defined, and this creates an opportunity to manage based on agreed expectations and standards."

(c)   Communications Solution

"As you know," says Nichols, "a major factor in the success of any organization is the extent of effective communication that exists between management and employees. This is no simple task and must be conducted in an open and honest environment. The presence of a union complicates this situation, by introducing the need to communicate with a third party, which in many cases has divergent opinions on many management issues. In many cases it's a "them-or-us" environment, which does not foster effective communications."

He offers a workable answer to this problem. "The only effective way to solve this problem," he says, "is to work with the union in forging a true partnership. Management cannot go to the union with only management issues. It must also work with the union on its interests and problems. The union, on the other hand, must recognize that effective management of an organization is a valuable and essential function, and have a clear understanding of the economic and other business realities that the organization is facing."

Solum sees the situation in the same light. "Management and the union have agreed," he explains, "that it is in their mutual interest to work in an environment where there is labor/management peace and cooperation. This enables us to meet competitive challenges, secure economic security for the employees, and better serve our customers. Management and the union will attempt to settle matters of mutual interest such as environmental concerns, individual safety, and administrative matters in the spirit of the partnership."

Nichols concludes that, as a start, both parties should separately define their goals for the organization and then come together and compare the two objectives. "In most cases you will be surprised to learn how similar the goals are. A longer-range objective in a true partnership is to involve the union in defining the strategic business plans for the organization."

(d) The Technology Issue

"One of the challenges we've been trying to address," says another innovative accounts payable manager, "is convincing the union and our HR department that there is a difference between typing and data entry. The clerks are given typing aptitude tests, but are not tested for data entry ability." Part of that company's solution is to work with a local community college in creating a half-day data entry course.

That is not the only technology-related issue this professional faces. In addition there are all the usual issues of productivity, motivation, customer service, and so on to be dealt with. "As we install new processes and systems ('new' meaning work traditionally not done by union clerks), we staff the new roles with nonunion personnel. This is usually at a lower rate and can provide greater flexibility and control over the work. We have been able to steadily improve our services over the last few years this way (and often it is one of the union members who gets the job)."

(e) Motivation Issues

Most managers use money as a motivational tool. Rewarding good performance with a larger salary increase is one way managers encourage good employees. Whether this actually works is a debate for another time. The fact is that when dealing with unions where pay rates are negotiated collectively, money can be less effective as a motivational tool. So, what do managers do? Solum and Nichols explained how they still manage to get good performance when money is no longer the object.

"Pay is negotiated," says Solum, "and there is no variable or incentive compensation plan for the work that is performed. In most cases, a union shop has a competitive pay rate. We established productivity and quality expectations that were negotiated and agreed to by the union. This provides each employee with a clear understanding of the company's expectations." He has hit the nail on the head. Many experts advise that setting clear expectations is a good way to motivate and communicate with employees.

Nichols offers some additional thoughts. "While money is certainly important," he says, "I have found four major motivational issues in my discussions with employees concerning the workplace of the future." Good management/employee relationships require that a company:

1. Aim for balance in work and personal life.
2. Respect employees for what they do and who they are.
3. Involve employees in the decisions that affect their work.
4. Empower employees to make the decisions that will get the job done.

His advice would certainly work for all accounts payable staffers, be they union employees or not.

(f)   Special Accommodations

Companies must run their operations a little differently when the accounts payable departments are staffed with union employees. Solum explains how Southern California Gas Company handles the issues. "A shop committee has been established," he says, "to deal with matters concerning the represented employees. In that context, union and management deal with matters that are strictly local to the department and that do not involve changes to the agreement or company policy. Issues that are not resolved may be transferred to the regular grievance procedure."

Nichols faced some additional challenges. Specifically, training and performance documentation required special considerations. Here's how he addressed the issues.

- *Training:* The introduction of new technology in the accounts payable operation was sometimes met with resistance by some employees. "Most of this resistance came from our longer service employees, and it was difficult to differentiate those who were intimidated by the new technology from those who were simply resisting change. The union continuously questioned our generic training programs as new technology was being introduced, resulting in the need for extensive additional training costs before we could clearly identify those employees who were not in favor of change."

- *Performance Documentation:* The presence of a union required a more comprehensive and structured approach for documenting poor performance. Although productivity standards were in place, there was not automatic agreement between management and the union as to what constituted cause to terminate an employee.

(g) Concluding Thoughts

No accounts payable manager gets to choose between working in a union or a nonunion shop; it is or is not a fact of life. Those faced with the challenge need to adapt and adapt quickly. "Hang in there," advises an accounts payable professional who effectively manages union staff. "Learn to deal with the situation and make it work. It can be done. Learn and understand the union contract and the various rules that apply. Find ways that you can recognize and reward the good workers without violating the contract. Your options may be limited, but among them you should be able to find the solution you're looking for."

He also suggests that managers work with the union when appropriate or necessary, but work directly with the people whenever possible. "Most of the people really want to do a good job," he points out, "and take pride in their work. While you're focusing on the small percentage of the staff that doesn't want to do the work, don't lose sight of the majority who really are trying to contribute."

8

Staff Motivation
and Morale

p. 97. Insert at end of chapter:

8.7 A REALISTIC APPROACH TO ACCOUNTS PAYABLE STAFF MOTIVATION (NEW)

When BankBoston's Steve Monaco began his talk at RECAP's Enhancing Accounts Payable conference, *Motivating People: A Business Perspective,* he said that not everyone would agree with his approach. After hearing the lecture, we believe that few will disagree with his reasonable approach.

(a) Why Motivate?

Most accounts payable managers want some recognition of the contributions they make to the company, a well-deserved pat on the back, an ever-increasing paycheck, and upward mobility, according to Monaco—although not necessarily in that order. He says that for managers to achieve these goals, they must motivate their employees. He provided a telling quote from a famous person (himself): "Managers are nothing without their staff."

Most managers motivate in one of two ways. Some use the "touchy-feely" (to use Monaco's definition) approach, which is extremely understanding of all employees' shortcomings and mistakes, regardless of responsibility. At the other extreme are those hard-line managers who demand unreasonable things from their employees and are never satisfied with the work produced. The trick, says Monaco, is to find a balance between the two extremes. He breaks the basics of motivation into four categories: respect, communication, accountability, and leadership.

(b) Respect

He says that respect is a balance between fear and love. While fear is a great motivator in the short term, it eventually erodes and undercuts respect and productivity. Love works well in the short term but is shattered by the need to make hard decisions. Monaco believes that respect is achieved through a balance of understanding and fairness.

He recommends that accounts payable managers begin by realizing that employees need to achieve the same desires as the manager. He also suggests that accounts payable managers begin to understand some of the personal circumstances that employees face as individuals. This is an area that some managers overlook. He gives the simple example of the need of some employees to leave early on October 31 to take their children trick-or-treating. By recognizing obligations such as this and finding ways to help the employee meet this requirement, the accounts payable manager goes a long way toward earning their respect.

Monaco is quick to point out that he does not mean to imply that every employee be given time off every time it is requested because there is another issue—the little matter of fairness. He says that this is tricky but the accounts payable manager must also measure the fairness of the decision in how other employees are affected by it. It is important that the same employee does not get all the "best" days off while others are relegated to the time no one wants. He does not believe in giving time off based on seniority but rather a fair sharing of the preferred days.

(c) Communication

There is probably not a manager alive who has not heard complaints about "lack of communication." Monaco says that although this is a battle most accounts payable managers will never win, they should also never stop trying. He believes that constant communication is important to staff motivation. He says it should be regular and honest.

The communication should be at all levels of the department. He cautions managers that they should know the names of every single employee who reports to them. While this may be easy for those with small staffs, he is adamant that even those with large staffs should do the same.

Monaco believes that employees are an accounts payable manager's most valuable asset. Therefore, regular communication meetings should never be cancelled. He takes regular communication meetings one step further. He invites guest speakers to help his staff grow and learn. The lecturer can be someone from another department or someone who will teach the group a new skill.

While many accounts payable managers can get the regular part of the communication down pat, the honest part is more difficult. Delivering bad or unpleasant news is never easy and something that most avoid if they can. Keep in mind that not telling the employees anything can be worse than telling them the truth. If the manager does not tell them, they will deduce it and often infer matters far worse than the actual news. Even worse, they might hear the news from another source, decimating morale in the process. Thus, the old adage "honesty is the best policy" applies more than ever when the news is bad.

(d) Accountability

This is probably the trickiest part of Monaco's motivation theory. He points out the following two factors often overlooked when running a department:

1. The company is in business to make money for the shareholders.
2. Employees have been hired and are paid to do a job.

He believes in setting expectation standards for employees. He says that some may not agree with him but if an accounts payable manager is to be successful in helping the company meet its objectives, the following must be done:

- Expectation standards must be set.
- Performance measures must be established and used.
- Rewards must be given when performance goals are achieved.

What Monaco is talking about is benchmarking operations. He says that this is important so that maximum productivity can be attained while ensuring fairness to all employees. He believes that the standards should be realistic but challenging and that the targets should be set for all employees. Thus, when a target is set for the number of invoices to be processed in a day is established, it should be set for all employees. Of course, a company that has invoices of different complexity might set the standard not on number of invoices, but number of lines (on invoices) handled. This would eliminate the possibility of having some employees handle "easier" invoices, leaving the more difficult ones to the more productive workers.

Having established departmental performance measures, each individual's performance can be measured against this standard. Some accounts payable managers post results by individual for everyone in the department to see.

Monaco believes that the employee's actual performance can be used to reward employees appropriately. He says that the employee who does nothing gets nothing at raise time. He also believes that giving flat raises is bad for departmental morale and productivity. After all, if the poorest-performing employee gets the same salary increase as the one who goes above and beyond, what incentive is there to really push?

Additionally, the benchmarking results identify those areas where corrective action needs to be taken. In the extreme, if the employee does not take the corrective action steps, the accounts payable manager then has the necessary support to begin termination proceedings. In extreme cases, Monaco does believe in letting nonproductive staffers go.

(e)   Leadership

"Leadership," says Monaco, "is a combination of respect, communication and accountability." All are aspects of leadership. He strongly believes in pay for performance and says that it is possible to implement such a strategy in all organizations—even those with union shops. This is the vision that Monaco sees for the future.

* 8.8   IMPROVING THE IMAGE OF ACCOUNTS PAYABLE (NEW)

Encouraging or requiring accounts payable associates to read general management books is one way to broaden staff knowledge. One savvy accounts payable supervisor not only requires her staff to read these books, but she's also found a pretty nifty way to let management know about it. Diane Gee, accounts payable supervisor at Systems and Electronics Inc., bought the book *Who Moved My Cheese,* by Spencer Johnson and Ken Blanchard (Putnam Publishing Group, 1998), for the staff to read. When each person finishes the book (it's fairly short), he or she signs the book, either on the inside of the front or back cover. Then Gee lends the book to various members of senior management, who, intrigued by all the signatures, look to see who has read it. While this one step alone won't improve management's perception of the staff, it is one of the many small things managers can do to gradually change management's perception of the staff.

9

Working with/for Purchasing and Other Departments

p. 111. Insert new sections:

9.5 CAN A/P AND PURCHASING REALLY WORK TOGETHER? (NEW)

The future is changing rapidly for accounts payable professionals; technology, the Internet, reengineering initiatives, and management expectations are all having an impact. By understanding these changes, accounts payable professionals will be able to prepare themselves for the new world order in A/P. We have identified three trends that will radically transform the face of accounts payable departments:

1. Joining payables and purchasing in one department.
2. Redefining the work of accounts payable professionals from transactional to analytical and control.
3. Hiring better-educated and better-trained individuals to handle the functions that fall under the accounts payable umbrella.

(a) Payables and Purchasing Together

A growing number of companies have reengineered their procurement-to-pay cycle to eliminate non–value-added functions. This trend is the subject of "Solutions for Procurement and Payables Excellence," a paper presented at the National Association of Procurement Professionals (NAPP) annual conference. This organization actively recruited payables professionals to attend its conference!

Managers in both payable and purchasing attended the event. In fact, as an indication of just how much the field is changing, many procurement managers invited the accounts payable managers from their organizations to join them at the conference. Approximately half the sessions were joint, with the remaining divided into breakout sections devoted to topics of special interest to each group.

(b) Transactional versus Analytical

One of the breakout sessions was an accounts payable managers' forum. The group's accounts payable advisor, Barbara Kuryea of Barbara R. Kuryea Consulting Services, led the session.

P-cards, e-catalogs (electronic online catalogs), and electronic data interchange (EDI) over the Internet are all reducing the volume of invoices running through accounts payable. The result is often, but not always, positive. With fewer transactions to process, the groups are becoming more analytical and control-oriented. Many in the group were optimistic about the future, seeing a gradual shift from data entry to audit and control as the main focus for accounts payable.

One of the accounts payable professionals in the group was worried by the trend, however. He sees many companies cutting their accounts payable staffs to the bone and is concerned that accounts payable departments will be lost in the shuffle.

Not everyone sees the future this way. A representative from one of the accounts payable audit firms indicated that she did not see a shift away from high levels of transactional processing happening with many of her clients.

(c)   Higher-Level Accounts Payable Departments

Those departments that manage to move away from data entry toward an analytical and control model will, of course, need either to retrain their existing staff or hire better-educated and better-trained professionals. To attract and retain highly skilled workers, as required in the new workplace, will necessitate higher salaries—and that is where many accounts payable managers have a problem.

"We have no trouble attracting skilled entry-level staff," reported one accounts payable manager from a well-known company at the NAPP, "but they leave for better-paying jobs the first opportunity they get." She is lucky to get six months out of her new hires, she said. If management is serious about retaining a highly skilled staff in accounts payable, salaries will have to rise.

This means sprucing up the department's image, getting grade levels raised, and getting management to realize the value that accounts payable adds to the company. These are not necessarily tasks at which accounts payable professionals excel. Tooting their own horn does not come naturally to most in the accounts payable profession. However, they must do so if they want to attract the kind of notice that accompanies higher-grade levels, titles, and salaries.

Recognizing these trends is the first step for the professional who wants to succeed in the brave new world of accounts payable. Once they are identified, managers can then take the necessary steps to ready themselves and their departments for the upcoming changes.

The NAPP has scheduled its next annual conference for January 2004. Check *www.nappconference.com.* Alternatively, contact Kuryea, the group's program director and accounts payable advisor, at *payables@aol.com.*

9.6   GETTING A CUSTOMER SERVICE MENTALITY IN A/P (NEW)

To improve departmental efficiency you need to develop a customer service mentality. The customers in this case are your employees.

Typically, this group includes those who submit T&E reports and check requests, purchasing managers who forward (and sometimes approve) POs and invoices for payment, and any other internal group that uses accounts payable's services.

Thomas F. Nichols, a consultant and president of Process Management Improvement, addressed this issue at RECAP's Enhancing Accounts Payable conference. Based on his 30-plus years with AT&T, he demonstrated how accounts payable professionals could become more customer service driven and improve departmental productivity.

(a) Case Study

When AT&T underwent a massive company-wide reengineering, the accounts payable department had to become more customer service driven or risk the business units taking their accounts payable business elsewhere. He met with his people and explained why change was necessary and the importance of acting quickly. He felt that it was better to act before there was any pressure from internal customers. He emphasized that what they had been doing was not wrong; it had simply outlived its usefulness.

He began by determining customers' level of satisfaction with the existing process, using a *Customer-Driven Organization Self-Assessment* survey. From that he was able to assess which customer requirements were not being met. It is important that readers concerned about customer satisfaction complete a similar survey on a periodic basis, first to benchmark where they are and then to measure improvements.

He also established negotiating teams to handle the initial service agreements with each of the units. When both parties agree on the service parameters, dissatisfaction is less likely to arise. The business units were most concerned with the following five issues: accuracy, cost, timeliness, service, and customer value-added services.

(b) The People

Since Nichols was asking his staff to change a lot, he thought it only fair to inquire about what they wanted. Their responses suggest that most accounts payable staffers want:

- A balance between work and their personal life
- Respect for what they do and who they are
- Involvement in the decisions that affect their work
- Empowerment to make the decisions needed to get the job done
- Flexibility to change when circumstances are altered

Believing their requests to be reasonable, Nichols worked their wishes into the organizational structure whenever and wherever possible.

(c) Customer Satisfaction

In order to measure whether a customer satisfaction program is working, Nichols says it is necessary to measure the results on a regular basis. To make sure his staff understood how important customer satisfaction was, he tied a portion of their bonuses to the results of a customer satisfaction survey. He says that companies that do not have bonus programs for their accounts payable staff can base portions of their annual raises on the results.

He used a *Customer Satisfaction Report Card* to measure customer satisfaction annually. He says that he did not expect his group to score 100%, but he looked to see an improvement each year over the prior year.

What Nichols did at AT&T is an excellent roadmap for accounts payable professionals today, especially those under pressure to do more with less and to address the concerns of other departments. Accounts payable professionals will find that by becoming more customer service driven and by reviewing the suggestions on the report card, they will be able to structure their workflow to address customers' concerns. They will simultaneously improve the department's standing with upper management.

(d) Customer Service Guidelines

A number of factors should be analyzed when checking to see where an accounts payable department stands with regard to customer service. A few that Nichols finds particularly important are listed below along with relevant features.

1. **Accuracy**
   - *Use purchasing summary reports* to highlight differences between invoices and POs.
   - *Put controls in place* to handle problems when paying from a copy of the invoice.
   - *Change processes* to enable a more timely update to the master vendor file.
   - *Conduct* annual internal audit reviews.
   - *Utilize* third-party audit firms.

2. **Cost**
   - *Establish a task-oriented costing team* to develop pricing strategies and price all invoice rework. One of the results of this effort at AT&T was to establish the cost for a manual check at $150.
   - *Create a quality program* using workflow diagrams and Pareto charts.
   - *Set up* a benchmarking team.

3. **Timeliness**
   - *Set an internal goal* of five days for processing a paper invoice.
   - *Set a policy* of taking discounts only if earned.

- *Request justification* in those cases where invoices were sent directly to the client, affecting your company's ability to take discounts.

4. **Service**

- *Put better people* in the inquiry lines.
- *Implement* an interactive voice response system.
- *Align* processing teams with the business units.

5. **Customer Value-Added Services**

- *Leverage* non-PO procurements.
- *Take an aggressive approach* to reporting bypasses to both purchasing and the business units.
- *Arrange for an analysis* of telecommunications payments.
- *Review* lease management.

Part Three

Management Issues

10

Master Vendor Files

10.2 CLEAN-UP POLICIES

p. 116. Add the following after fifth sentence of paragraph:

See Exhibit 10.3A for this information further broken down by the size of the company; Exhibit 10.3B is broken down by industry.

p. 117. Delete Exhibit 10.2 and replace with the following:

Exhibit 10.2 **How Many Vendors Should Be in Your Vendor File?**

Number of Vendors	Percentage of Companies
Less than 1,000	12.5
1,000–5,000	41.6
5,001–20,000	29.1
20,001–100,000	4.3
More than 100,000	2.0

Source: IOMA.

p. 117. Insert after carryover material:

10.2A WHEN TO SET UP A NEW FILE (NEW)

Accounts payable managers must find a balance between setting up new vendor files and keeping the miscellaneous vendor file from getting unmanageable. The point at which a vendor *qualifies* for its own file can generate considerable controversy. Six veteran accounts payable pros recently tackled the issue on the IOMA accounts payable discussion group.

(a) The Issue

"I have been asked by my controller to 'thin' my vendor miscellaneous files. Currently I have a five-drawer file cabinet that contains the paid invoices for the present year. Earlier this year I created new files for vendors with 10 or more invoices in the miscellaneous file. My controller thinks new vendor files should be created when a vendor has more than three invoices. She feels this will be more convenient for her research purposes. I'm looking to see how other accounts payable handle this issue. I feel that the file should be maintained for my convenience because I use these files daily," writes a weary accounts payable manager.

(b) Majority Opinion

In this case, the accounts payable professionals are in sync with management. Here are how a few of them explained their reasoning:

- "I've always made a new file for vendors that exceed more than three invoices in the miscellaneous file. I use this file for those vendors that maybe get paid once a year or so. If there are already three invoices for the one vendor, then, more than likely, there will be other invoices to follow. It makes looking them up much easier."
- "I manage the accounts payable department for a large financial institution. We create new vendor files for vendors

over three invoices also. Research is easier that way. It is more efficient to create the file than trying to find invoices in a three-inch-thick miscellaneous file."

- "Seems that three invoices are the general consensus! I am the accounts payable manager for a mid-sized telecommunications company, and we also create a separate file for any vendor to which we pay three invoices."

- "We used to create new files for vendors with more than three invoices. Now we set up files for each vendor. Truthfully, we all prefer the lengthier system of having a file for each and every vendor."

(c)   Minority Point of View

There were a few dissident votes. Not everyone felt three invoices were appropriate. Here are what two other accounts payable professionals had to say on this issue:

- "We do very few miscellaneous vendors since these are much harder to track. All our vendors are set up in the master file. This gives us the ability to run a search in our check disbursement file for those payments, even if there has only been one."

- "There is no one correct answer for filing, but for whatever it is worth I work for a $250 million sales per year company, and we do not use miscellaneous vendor files. All vendors are fully established in our accounting system (Oracle). We file payments by payment number, which these days are mostly electronic."

As the last participant indicated, there may be no correct answer. What works in one organization may not work in the next. Still, the information provided by the majority will serve as a guideline to those forced to make a decision at their own companies.

p. 118. *Delete existing Exhibit 10.3 and replace with the following:*

Exhibit 10.3 **Timing of Master Vendor File Clean-Up**

Monthly	4.2%
Quarterly	2.9%
Yearly	32.2%
Every 2 years	16.6%
Every 3 years	16.8%
Never	27.2%

Source: IOMA.

p. 118. *Insert after Exhibit 10.3:*

Exhibit 10.3A **Timing of Master Vendor File Clean-Up by Size of Company**

	Monthly	Quarterly	Yearly	Every 2 Years	Every 3 Years	Never
Up to 99	5.3	1.8	35.1	10.5	14.0	33.3
100–249	1.6	7.1	32.3	17.3	13.4	28.3
250–499	4.2	2.5	31.4	14.4	16.1	31.4
500–999	3.9	1.6	27.9	19.4	22.5	24.8
1,000–4,999	4.2	2.1	31.2	18.0	16.4	28.0
Over 5,000	8.8	2.7	27.7	15.0	15.0	25.7

Source: IOMA.

Exhibit 10.3B   **Timing of Master Vendor File Clean-Up by Industry**

	Monthly	Quarterly	Yearly	Every 2 Years	Every 3 Years	Never
Manufacturing	5.5	2.0	28.1	14.6	18.6	31.2
Finance	7.9	6.3	38.1	19.0	12.7	15.9
Utilities, transportation	6.4	4.3	29.8	10.6	21.3	27.7
Private practice	1.8	1.8	41.8	10.9	20.0	23.6
Nonprofit	0	0	38.5	15.4	12.8	33.3
Wholesale/retail/ distribution	4.7	3.1	33.3	19.4	8.5	31.0
Health care	2.7	2.7	39.7	20.3	27.0	17.6
Education	3.8	7.7	26.9	7.7	15.4	38.5
Media	2.8	5.6	30.6	16.7	22.2	22.2
Construction	9.1	4.5	40.9	27.3	4.5	13.6
Entertainment/ hospitality	0	0	31.9	23.2	14.5	29.0

Source: IOMA.

p. 118. Insert after first full paragraph, before heading:

10.4A   ESTABLISHING VENDOR NAMING CONVENTIONS (NEW)

Due to the lack of a standard vendor naming convention, many companies end up with more than one file for the same vendor. The result is duplicate payments. It is not unusual to find vendor files for IBM, I.B.M., International Business Machine, I B M, and so on, at the same company.

The important issue when considering a vendor naming policy is that it be consistent. To help readers establish vendor naming guidelines at their own organizations, we present a sample naming policy from RECAP, Inc. Modify it to fit your own requirements. To do so, RECAP recommends answering the following seven questions:

1. How many characters does your system allow for a vendor name?

2. Does your system allow more than one line for a vendor name?

3. Does your system allow for a different name to appear on the check than on a 1099?

4. Can you look up a vendor based on a short name, full name, or "sounds like"?

5. When you look up a vendor and a list of vendors is displayed, how much of the vendor's name and address are displayed so that you can select the correct vendor?

6. Are there limits as to how many characters/lines of a name can be printed on checks, fed to other systems, appear on reports or screens, appear in window envelopes or on labels used for mailings?

7. Can you link vendors under a common identifier with an address qualifier to allow multiple addresses for the same vendor?

With the answers to these questions and the policy suggested in subsection (a), you will be able to devise a naming policy for your company that will eliminate duplicate files for the same vendor.

(a)   Sample Naming Policy

- If the name is a corporation that includes Corp., Inc., or LLC, include that in the name when you set up the vendor.

- If the name of the vendor begins with an article (*The, A,* etc.), do not include it in the name when you set up the vendor.

- If the name is an individual, consistently include or exclude prefixes such as Mr., Ms., or Dr.

- Avoid using periods (.) within vendor names and use one space after each initial.

- Avoid using apostrophes in vendor names or in abbreviations of words in vendor names.

- Avoid abbreviations or be consistent in their use.

- Vendor names beginning with a number should be entered as specified. However, names that begin with a year, such as the 1999 U.S. Open, and are likely to be used again for another year should be set up without the year prefix.

- If abbreviations are used, a short table of allowable abbreviations should be prepared and provided to people who are authorized to add vendors, as well as to people who have to find vendors based on a name. For example, American can be abbreviated either Am or Amer. Decide which you will use and include it in the list.

- If the vendor is *doing business as, trading as,* or *known as,* use the vendor's actual name and DBA, TA, or KA, followed by that name on the second line of "name" or first line of the "address."

- If the vendor asks that you pay a factor, set up the name for the vendor and put the name of the factor as the second line of the name or the first line of the address.

- If the vendor is a taxing authority, set up the name of the taxing authority as the name. Put any qualifiers, such as department, division, and the like, on the second line of the name or on the first line of the address. Despite instruction on many property tax bills that specify that you make a check out to the name of an individual as tax collector, the check will be cashed if you make it out to the name of the taxing authority as the first part of the vendor's name.

- If your system does not support two-line names, consider using the first line of the address for the continuation of the vendor's name. If the vendor's name fits completely in the name field and the first line of the address is required, put a period in the first line of the address.

This policy is good, but so is any one that is consistent. Develop one that works for your own organization and then insist that everyone use it religiously.

p. 120. Insert new section before 10.6:

10.5A NEW VENDOR SET-UP (NEW)

One of the best ways to minimize duplicate payments and fraud is to have good controls on the master vendor file, and the time to start is when the vendor file is first set up. Unfortunately, this is the point where some companies have the fewest guidelines. When the vendor is set up, the requestor, most frequently someone from purchasing, scrawls some basic information on a piece of paper and leaves it for the accounts payable person in charge of setting up new vendors. Needless to say, organizations that have loose guidelines for establishing a new vendor are just as likely to be lax when changing a remit-to address—one of the easiest ways for an employee to perpetrate check fraud.

To help avoid these problems and to set up new vendors in a uniform manner, leading-edge companies use a *New Vendor Set-Up* form. Phillips International's Gary Bass has graciously shared his firm's form. It is shown in Exhibit 10.4. Readers can make copies for use in their own organizations. (Note: This form was set up in Word and can be easily replicated.)

Whether a company takes advantage of this form or uses one of its own creations, a vendor set-up form will reduce the chances of both duplicate payments and fraud. Who can argue against that?

Exhibit 10.4   **New Vendor Set-Up Form**

COMPANY #: _____   NEW VENDOR: [   ]

                                     NEW REMIT: [   ]

VENDOR ID: _____

VENDOR NAME: _____
(The check payable name)

VENDOR ADDRESS: _____

_____

CITY: _____ STATE: _____ ZIP CODE: _____

TERMS: _____

ONE CHECK PER INVOICE: YES: _____ NO: _____

PHONE #: _____

VENDOR GROUP: _____ (please see the list of vendor group below)

VENDOR TYPE: Please Check One.

Corporation: [   ]   FED ID #: _____

Employee: [   ]   (Not needed)

1099 Vendor: [   ]   Soc Sec #: _____

Submitted by: _____

Approved by: _____

Vendor group list:

ACQ	Acquisitions	ADV	Advertising	RNT	Rent
CON	Consultant	GEN	General		
CTB	Contribution	P/M	Printing/Mailing		
TEL	Telephone	PST	Postage		
TMP	Temporary Help	ROY	Royalties		

p. 122. Insert new section:

10.9   VENDOR FILE BEST PRACTICES (NEW)

Vendor practices—including the management of new vendors, the master vendor file, data from the vendor files, and the application of vendors' payments—are typically the key areas to look at when setting up best A/P practices. Speaking at a special workshop following the IOMA/IMI Managing Accounts Payable conference, RECAP's Jon Casher showed attendees how to manage these areas most efficiently.

(a)   Best Vendor Management Practices

Good vendor practices start at the beginning when a new vendor is first brought on board. To avoid obvious cases of fraud, Casher recommends verifying that the vendor is legitimate. While this may seem obvious, more than a few companies omit this step. How can you check the company out? One way is to check the phone book or one of the business databases. This can be done with a few clicks of a mouse on the Internet.

To avoid year-end 1099 problems, send out substitute W-9 forms. Should the vendor "forget" to return the form, you can hold up payment until the form is completed and returned (assuming management concurs with this strategy).

Each new vendor should be sent a welcome package setting out accounts payable policies and procedures as they affect the vendor. This practice lays the groundwork for a good working relationship and closes the door on those "nobody ever told me" excuses.

Casher also strongly recommends purging the master vendor file every year. Without this action, it becomes unwieldy. Additionally, the file should be cleaned up to eliminate duplicate entries in the file for the same vendor. Duplicate entries are one of the leading causes of duplicate payments.

One of the best ways to make sure you do not enter the same vendor twice in the master vendor file is to use standard rules for names. By using standard rules, you do not end up with entries for IBM and I.B.M., for example. Casher also recommends using the post office's rules for addresses. This limits duplicate entries into

the master vendor file. He says that accounts payable professionals should capture phone numbers and other appropriate information when the master vendor file is being set up. Some accounts
payable professionals also record e-mail addresses.

Finally, he says, apply the appropriate strategy to your master vendor files in all instances.

(b)   The Vendor File

Casher recommends having a strategy to verify the vendor before
doing business with a new firm. That approach will depend on the
nature of your business and the part the new vendor will play in
your production cycle. If the vendor is small and the product supplied nonstrategic, the verification process described above may
be sufficient. If the new vendor is strategic or is to supply a large
quantity of material, then your company may want to do a credit
check or obtain references. Often, but not always, this responsibility falls under the purchasing umbrella.

Policies regarding vendor set-up and changes should be
firmly established. Casher suggests that the corporate vendor policy should set out:

- Who decides to add a vendor.
- What checks are done before a new vendor is added and
  what forms are required.
- Vendor naming conventions.
- Vendor address standards.
- What data will be captured in the vendor file.
- Policies to deal with one-time vendors.

Similarly, there should be a corporate policy regarding the
purging of the master vendor file. At a minimum, it should address:

- How long inactive vendors are kept on file.
- How often the master is purged.
- Criteria for purging a vendor.
- What records are kept for purged vendors.

While purging the master vendor file may seem obvious to
many reading this, not all companies attend to the task. Over 30%

of companies of all sizes (and almost 33% of the largest companies) admitted in the most recent IOMA *Benchmarking Accounts Payable* survey that they never purge their master vendor files.

(c) Using Vendor Information

The vendor files and related data hold a treasure trove of information for those who know how to use it accurately. At the workshop, Casher asked attendees a series of questions. Those who can gather the answers to these questions will be able to make the most of the data both in efficiently managing their department and for negotiation of better prices and terms. Here are the questions:

1. Do you eliminate duplicate vendors?
2. Do you link related vendors?
3. Do you capture Tax ID and 1099 category data?
4. Do you know which of your vendors are women or minority owned? How about small business owners?
5. Do you analyze where, with whom, and on what your company spends its money?
6. Can you identify top vendors by dollars spent?
7. Can you identify top vendors by transaction volume?

The answers to these questions will arm the accounts payable professional with the information needed to play a crucial role within the organization. What are you going to do next?

Casher had two additional pieces of information regarding vendor payments. He runs an accounts payable audit company, so he knows how to find the traps accounts payable typically falls into. Here is what he recommends:

1. Request and review vendor statements. When asking for those statements, stipulate that you want them to include all activity, including credits.
2. Do self-audits and follow-up with third-party audits. Follow the recommendations made by the auditors.

Following Casher's recommendations will not only save your company money, it may also get management to look at you in a new light—and it's about time.

Part Four

Travel and Entertainment

15

Handling Employee Travel and Entertainment Reports

15.3   HOW MUCH CHECKING IS ENOUGH?

p. 171. Delete existing Exhibit 15.1 and replace with:

Exhibit 15.1   **What Level of Checking Do You Use for T&E?**

	Spot Check (%)	Moderate Check (%)	In-Depth Check (%)
	18.6	27.6	53.8
By Size of Company	Spot Check (%)	Moderate Check (%)	In-Depth Check (%)
Up to 99	25.0	25.0	50.0
100–249	17.8	28.8	53.4
250–499	13.5	30.6	55.9
500–999	15.7	26.0	58.3
1,000–4,999	17.6	26.9	55.5
Over 5,000	25.2	30.1	44.7

Source: IOMA.

p. 172. Delete existing Exhibit 15.2 and replace with:

Exhibit 15.2   Level of Checking by Industry

By Industry	Spot Check (%)	Moderate Check (%)	In-Depth Check (%)
Manufacturing	18.6	24.6	56.8
Finance	14.8	29.5	55.7
Utilities, transportation	26.5	34.7	38.8
Private practice	11.5	23.1	65.4
Nonprofit	9.1	24.2	66.7
Wholesale/retail/distribution	24.4	34.1	41.5
Health care	19.4	31.9	48.6
Education	12.0	24.0	64.0
Media	31.4	17.1	51.4
Construction	20.0	25.0	55.0
Entertainment/hospitality	5.3	15.8	78.9
Other	15.9	27.0	57.1

Source: IOMA.

p. 178. Insert new section:

15.8   HOW YOU CAN KEEP A LID ON T&E EXPENSES (NEW)

Given the downturn in the economy, companies looking to cut costs will almost inevitably focus on their second largest controllable expenditure. A recent survey of corporate travel managers confirms this view. Runzheimer International's latest report shows that 54% of the companies it surveyed have reduced domestic travel expenditures, while 26% have cut expenses associated with international travel. The respondents shared the details of exactly how they reduced these expenses.

Companies that reported reducing corporate travel did so overwhelmingly by taking drastic steps; they cut the number of trips taken almost across the board. Every company that reduced travel expenses cut the number of international trips, while 96% of them slashed the number of domestic trips.

(a)   International versus Domestic Trips

At first glance, one might expect international travel to provide at least the same reduction as domestic travel, if not more. After all, international travel is vastly more expensive. Closer scrutiny reveals something different, however.

People generally do not undertake an international business trip unless it is absolutely necessary. The expense of the trip, the time away from the office, and the logistical conflicts associated with these trips often make them an option only in extreme cases. Making courtesy calls on customers located a few hours away is a nice gesture; making them to customers a few time zones away is an expensive expenditure many companies feel they can live without.

(b)   How Travel Has Changed

Next on the chopping block, at least domestically, were conferences and seminars. Almost two-thirds of those reducing expenses either reduced or eliminated attendance at these events, while only 42% cut attendance at international conferences. There was an interesting exception to this trend. Attendance at the recent Association of Corporate Travel Executives was up. Experts theorize that companies sent their travel pros in record numbers because they wanted them to find ways to reduce travel costs.

First-class travel took a larger hit internationally, reflecting the fact that a number of companies permit first-class travel on international trips but not domestically. Internationally, approvals are being sought more frequently than in the past. The theory behind this requirement is that if a discussion with a supervisor is held before the trip is planned, a less expensive alternative, such as videoconferencing, may be selected.

(c)   What Else?

Innovative managers are always searching for ways to cut T&E costs. With the pressure turned on, many are finding innovative ways to reduce their expenditures. We warn you that not all may be to your management's liking. Review the selections but, before implementing any of them, make sure to get management's approval. You will need it when you break the news to traveling employees.

There is one late-breaking place that savvy travel pros may be able to save their companies some serious dollars. Hotels across the nation have been reporting lower occupancy rates, even in major cities. Those companies with negotiating clout may be able to renegotiate existing contracts to take advantage of the hotels' desire to fill their rooms. This might also be an excellent time to approach chains where no existing relationship exists.

When talking to the hotels, make sure that the negotiators focus not only on the room price, but also on those pesky energy surcharges, which can really add up. In addition, if the hotels have been adding luxury charges, resort charges, or some other nonsense to the bills of your travelers, this can be addressed now.

Finally, even if the hotels won't budge on their prices, you may be able to get them to throw in some extra perks for your travelers. Since many busy business travelers make extensive use of the Internet hookup in their rooms, getting the hotel to throw that in for free would save most companies some money.

More than a few employees would appreciate the use of the hotel gym or spa without having to pay $10 or $15 or more per day for that privilege—money that often comes out of the employees' own pocket. Gaining these small benefits makes selling some of the other cost-saving initiatives just a little easier.

Between management support and the possibility of adding a benefit or two when asking employees to reduce travel costs, T&E pros will have some help when trying to reduce T&E expenditures.

16

Electronic Travel and Entertainment Handling

p. 185. *Insert new section:*

16.4 E-TICKETS (NEW)

If your company's travelers are using e-tickets, chances are that some of the cost savings are going down the drain. That's because travelers who change their flights at the last minute can easily forget to cash in unused tickets.

True, unused airline tickets have always been a problem. However, with e-tickets, there is no physical piece of paper to remind travelers to get the refund. Therefore, the problem—and your potential cash loss—is worse than ever. American Express says that more than 4% of e-tickets issued by corporate travel departments go unused. Fortunately, new systems have emerged to track unused e-tickets, and even process refunds; however, many companies are unaware of these systems.

(a) A Leading Automated Solution: Ticket TRAX

A leading provider of e-ticket tracking software solutions is:

- *Ticket TRAX (www.americanexpress.com).* If your company is an American Express Business Travel client, you can use

Ticket TRAX, which was unveiled in 2000. You pay for this service by giving American Express a cut of what they recover. In the first four months of in-market trials, Ticket TRAX identified and refunded more than $2.5 million in lost electronic tickets for 47 corporate clients, says American Express.

The nice part of this service is that no extra work is required from you or the traveler—Ticket TRAX takes care of the full refund process. The system logs a record of all electronic tickets booked by a corporation's employees through American Express Travel. It then checks the computer reservations systems (CRSs) after a specified period of time to determine if all segments of the ticket were used. Unlike most other electronic ticket refund services, Ticket TRAX can research tickets as far back as 13 to 22 months, depending on the data stored by the airline.

For each unused, refundable ticket, Ticket TRAX automatically initiates a refund request to the airline. It can also notify travelers by fax or e-mail to expect the refund, so they can correct their expense accounts. Ticket TRAX provides the travel manager with a monthly report documenting the amount of money Ticket TRAX has saved. Internal audit groups can use the report to help check expense reports.

(b)   Other Tracking Solutions

In addition to American Express, several other business travel agencies have e-ticket tracking solutions either currently in operation or in the works for their clients.

- *Airline Ticket Manager* (*www.interproexpense.com*). The software contains the Airline Ticket Manager feature, designed to help Expense Express users easily and properly report the disposition of airline tickets as they prepare their expense reports.

However, this system, unlike Ticket TRAX, relies on user input to track unused e-tickets. Therefore, it is not completely foolproof. Even so, users report big savings using this system. The system requires no additional time on the part of the traveler or your processing staff. Expense Express prompts users to indicate whether a ticket was used, unused, or partially used, and to submit any unused or partially used tickets to the company, along with other required receipts tied to that expense report.

Airline ticket information is screened through the system into Airline Ticket Manager and compiled into reports that can be used for reconciliation against charge card statements and to satisfy IRS audit requirements. The unused or partially used airline tickets are pulled from the expense report receipt packages and submitted for future travel credit.

- *ResTRACK (www.travelsys.com)*. Unlike Ticket TRAX and Airline Ticket Manager, ResTRACK can be used as a standalone system. Its provider, Automated Travel Systems, offers a full suite of automated solutions for corporate travel departments, including ResFAX, ResMAILrnet, ResMARKER, and ResQCX.

A strong feature of ResTRACK is its reporting capabilities. It has a self-generating reporting feature, and ad hoc reporting may also be accomplished via flat files imported to Crystal Report or Excel.

No additional keystrokes or formats are required to use ResTRACK. It analyzes all passenger name records (PNRs) containing an e-ticket indicator. Stored in its own database, ResTRACK will review e-ticket transactions at a specified interval after the last travel date in the itinerary. The user specifies the selection of two, five, or seven days after the last travel date. ResTRACK stops checking coupon status when a coupon is no longer "open."

- *eTrak (www.trondent.com)*. Similar to ResTRACK, eTrak (and eTrak Pro, an enhanced version) is a standalone product. eTrak is run at the end of each day and it reads the daily ticketing report in the CRS to obtain information about each e-ticket issued that day. This information is then stored in the eTrak database so that it can check final status of the flight coupons after travel is complete.

A nice feature of eTrak Pro is that it will update the traveler's profile with details of unused e-tickets, creating an alert for when the individual's next reservation is made.

Similar to ResTRACK, eTrak comes with a strong report module that offers several canned reports. It also allows for the use of Crystal Reports, Access, Excel, and Paradox. Currently eTrak offers five canned reports and more will be added soon. The existing reports are: All Tickets (both used and unused), Unused Segments Only, Unused Tickets Only (if one coupon is unused, entire ticket shows), Summary/Unused Segments, and Summary/Unused Tickets.

16A

Travel and Entertainment Automation (New)

Ask accounts payable managers what causes them the most grief and more than half will say the handling of travel and entertainment (T&E) reports. The "personal" nature of T&Es (especially in those organizations in which individuals pay the credit card balances themselves), combined with the highly intensive paper handling lead to this stress. Thus, anything that makes the process easier is welcome. Automation heads the list. This chapter looks at the automation processes being used to help facilitate this function. Many companies still insist on in-depth checking, which further impedes the process. Some ways leading-edge companies are automating the process are discussed in this chapter.

16A.1 MAKING THE MOST OF DIRECT DEPOSIT

Fair, Isaac, and Company Inc. has enjoyed a 95% or better participation in its direct-deposit program. Thus, their employees are accustomed to not receiving a check. "Most of our workforce travels and incurs reimbursable expenses at least occasionally," says David Warren, the company's accounts payable manager. "It has long been a source of complaints that we were unable to also give employees direct deposit for expense reimbursement," he explains.

The company was receiving requests from vendors to be paid either by wire transfer or through the automated clearinghouse (ACH). Fair, Isaac began searching for a quick solution in the summer of 1997. "We wanted to get a 'pretty good' solution in place quickly," says Warren, "rather than a more complete and expensive solution several years later."

He worked with a programmer and, where needed, several other employees. He talked to other companies in similar positions that had already implemented solutions. The company decided to use the standard Oracle payment processing to generate an output file and standard communication software and modem to send an ASCII file to the bank. An hour after the file is sent, he contacts the bank and downloads a results file. He says that throughout the process the company received good support from both BankAmerica and Oracle.

To test the new approach before going live company-wide, 20 volunteers were recruited from the finance department. The company ran test transactions for five weeks. These tests were for one cent plus any actual expense reimbursements. The company then added several dozen frequent traveler volunteers, and less than six months after the initial discussion, the system was introduced.

Initially, the company continued to provide the standard paper remittance advice for T&E reimbursements. It routed these through interoffice mail. When employees—especially those who traveled a good deal—complained, the company developed an e-mail notification system.

Application forms were also improved. They are now available on the Web. Warren hopes to eventually send the file to the bank via the Internet with the confirmation from the bank coming through e-mail. Is the program a success? "We currently have around 65% of our employee expense reimbursements using employee direct deposit," explains Warren. "We have had occasional problems with direct-deposit delivery. However, the requests for replacement checks vastly exceed the requests for direct-deposit replacements." The numbers speak for themselves.

16A.2   SPREADSHEET APPROACH

Not everyone who uses technology does so in a costly or complicated way. Many accounts payable professionals simply develop their own application using spreadsheets such as Excel or Lotus. "The best system I have seen belongs to Microsoft," says one accounts payable professional. "There were some rumors the company might sell this," she adds. A number of computer proficient accounts payable managers have created their own spreadsheets to handle their company's T&E processes. It is not difficult for those who have basic spreadsheet skills. If you or someone on your staff has the necessary computer skills, this might be an approach that would work in your company.

16A.3   LOTUS NOTES™

Lotus Notes works on the same lines as the Excel spreadsheet. "We have developed an expense account processing system within Lotus Notes," explains one accounts payable pro. "More than 95% of our expense accounts run through this process. We have added features such as credit card remittances, and so forth along the way. For 8,000 employees country-wide, this technique requires less than the equivalent of one full-time employee to support it from an information systems application perspective."

This approach demonstrates that it is possible for those with some computer savvy to develop customized applications that will handle their T&E requirements quite nicely. One does not have to be a technology whiz.

16A.4   ONE-CARD INTRANET-BASED SOLUTION

With over 100,000 employees in three countries using eight different credit cards for business purposes, General Motors' T&E processing was ripe for an innovative change. The company consolidated all employee corporate charge cards into a single, multifunctional card supported by one expense summary and management system. General Motors expects to reduce its costs by a whopping 93%, primarily by eliminating the costs associated with the handling of paper expense reports. To handle this business, General Motors chose Citibank, who teamed with Captura Software of Bothell, Washington, to provide a global intranet-based system.

"We're calling this new and innovative expense management solution a win-win-win," says Bill Wimsatt, General Motor's manager of accounting services. "It simplifies business travel and procedures for employees, and offers them a faster turn-around in expense reimbursement. . . . It saves the company a few million dollars a year; and it provides us with important financial information we can use to strengthen our leverage with suppliers in our corporate travel business," Wimsatt continued.

The new card offers General Motors and its employees many benefits. It will be intranet-based, so only those with approved passwords will be able to view information. All expense summaries will be filed electronically in the language and currency of the employee's local country. Since this new card will primarily be used in the United States, Mexico, and Canada, the languages available initially will be only English, Spanish, and French.

The new card greatly simplifies the life of the traveling executive. When employees access the secure intranet site, all charges made to their corporate card will already be visible in the system. Employees need only validate the charge card transaction by pointing and clicking.

The company benefits not only by the tremendous reduction in costs, but also by the new system's ability to aggregate data. The use of technology and this intranet-based solution allows General Motors to identify similar processes going on in different parts of the company. With this information, it identifies opportunities for huge savings and increased efficiencies.

16A.5 IN-HOUSE VERSUS THIRD PARTY

Like many of their peers, the professionals in the first two scenarios are reluctant to use one of the commercial products on the market because of expense. The initial price along with maintenance costs can be high. The price tag for developing an in-house system needs to be weighed carefully against the price of one of the third-party applications available. This is just the beginning of the analysis.

Many companies believe they can develop a customized system for their own T&E needs at a lower cost than those provided by a third party. However, with all the other technology priorities, getting the information systems (IS) resources allocated to accounts payable needs is often low on a company's priority list. Even if it can theoretically be done at a lower cost in-house, it is important to determine if and when the programmers will be available to work on the application.

Finally, it is necessary to determine how important improving T&E handling is at a company. If only a small number of employees actually travel, it will be difficult to make a case for either an expensive third-party solution or use of the company's limited IS resources. Accounts payable professionals who fall into this category might try and use their own skills to develop an acceptable module. By taking different pieces of the solutions discussed here, you may be able to develop something that will work in your company.

17

VAT Refunds

p. 189. *Insert after fourth full paragraph, before heading:*

17.3A   VAT FILING DEADLINES (NEW)

The deadlines for filing value-added tax (VAT) refunds can be confusing, as they are not all the same. Meridian VAT Reclaim *(www.meridianvat.com)* has prepared the following guidelines to assist readers in meeting VAT deadlines.

Canada has a "rolling deadline." Invoices must be submitted for refund within one year of the date that the invoice is issued. The European governments impose two filing deadlines: June 30 and December 31.

1. *United Kingdom:* The United Kingdom has separate filing deadlines for European Union (EU) and non–EU-based companies. EU-based companies must file by June 30 for expenses incurred in the United Kingdom during the previous calendar year. Non–EU-based companies must submit refund applications by December 31 for invoices dated July 1 of the previous year through June 30 of the current year.

2. *Rest of Europe:* June 30 is the deadline for all companies to file expenditures incurred between January 1 and

December 31 of the previous calendar year. *Note:* Belgium, the Netherlands, and Ireland allow one to file retroactive claims for invoices dating back several years.

Similar to most of Europe, the Korean government imposes a deadline of June 30, by which companies must file invoices for expenses incurred during the previous calendar year.

Accounts payable professionals who are aware of these dates can share them with their international travelers to ensure that they get the original invoices needed in a timely fashion. This enables accounts payable professionals to either apply for the refund or forward it to their VAT refund outsourcer before the deadline.

Part Five

High-Tech
Applications

18

Electronic Data Interchange

p. 214. Insert at bottom of page:

18.17A   WEB ELECTRONIC DATA INTERCHANGE: AN IDEA WHOSE TIME HAS COME (NEW)

"EDI promised you the moon," began Harris Bank's Hamish Forrest at a recent IOMA/IMI accounts payable conference. Forrest believes that many companies have found that their electronic data interchange (EDI) programs do not live up to the original expectations or the original business case. The theory sounded great and management teams across the country bought into the theory. In reality, however, it was quite different. Accounts payable professionals who were running the programs discovered that although they were EDI-capable, many of their trading partners were not.

This was due to cost, the inflexible nature of EDI, the non–user-friendliness of EDI, technology, and the fact that EDI was primarily a mainframe application. "Due to these gaps, plus a number of other critical issues," says Forrest, "companies have started to look at the Internet as an alternative means of delivering business documents." Consider the following three points:

1. Electronic commerce is growing and although it is primarily consumer-to-business applications now, by the year 2000, business-to-business commerce is expected to be 14 times larger than consumer-to-business.
2. By the year 2002, many experts estimate that business-to-business commerce over the Internet will exceed $300 billion.
3. By the year 2000, experts expect more than 80% of Canadian business and more than 50% of American business will either have access to or regularly use the Internet in their daily business life.

Thus, it appears that the technology is there, it is user-friendly enough, cost is not prohibitive, and the availability is within the reach of virtually any company that wants it. The limitations have been removed and, as the facts above indicate, most of a business's trading partners can use Web EDI. But will they? Recent research by Forrester Research shows that while 48% of the companies surveyed said they would not do EDI over the Internet today, 46% expect to in the next three years. "It will become the cost effective and accessible vehicle of choice as companies realize the Internet is probably the only way they will ever realize the benefits originally envisioned and promised from their EDI business case," concludes Forrest.

Harris Bank, as well as several other banks, offers a product that allows companies to do EDI over the Internet. To find out more, check its Web page at *www.totaltradepartners.com* or contact Forrest directly at 312-765-1198.

19A

Paying Cell Phone Bills (New)

Cellular phones are one technological advance that is causing accounts payable managers a great deal of grief. The problem is not just who will pay for them—it is much more complicated than that. In addition to the basic issue of who gets one and who does not, there are myriad charges associated with these devices, and it is not always clear which charges are business-related and which are personal. There is also the complication of sales and use tax issues. Finally, the situation is further aggravated by the fact that many cellular phone companies have not thought through all the fine points of the services they offer. The issue has been discussed among accounts payable professionals on the IOMA discussion group and elsewhere. The following is an overview of some of the problems encountered along with workable solutions.

19A.1 PROBLEM 1—NO POLICY

For starters, many companies do not have formal policies for cellular phones. Thus, many accounts payable professionals find themselves dealing with multiple contracts—all at different prices. Also, since there is no formal policy, some departments allow employees to have the phones while other departments do not.

"I'm arguing for a cellular phone policy that is similar to our travel reimbursement policy," writes one accounts payable professional on the IOMA discussion group. "The phone and the contract should be between the individual and the cellular phone company. The individual should pay the cellular phone company out of pocket and then submit a claim for reimbursement each month." How's he doing with this reasonable approach? "So far, I'm not succeeding, but I continue to wage the battle," he concludes.

Another participant in the discussion group reports that her company has a policy that states "base charges and business calls in excess of free minutes are reimbursable only if the company requires the employee to have a cell phone."

19A.2   PROBLEM 2—UNIFORM PRICING

In most organizations, extensive use by employees of cellular phones is so new that there is no uniform contract for everyone. Employees have gone out on their own to acquire their phones and contracts, but because some employees are better shoppers than others, the end result is chaos for the accounts payable staff trying to manage the process. While companies with no overall plan in place can start fresh, those with a variety of existing contracts will have a much harder time. Below is the way one company addressed that problem.

The company negotiated reduced corporate rates for cell phone charges with a large cellular provider in the Los Angeles area. The company also decided which plan to offer based on an average monthly call volume. It then offered the employee the option of purchasing a new digital phone (required for the reduced rate) at the employee's expense and being reimbursed at the reduced rate, or keeping their own cell phone and plan, and receiving a reimbursable expense not to exceed the corporate rate. Most employees bought a new cell phone and went with the corporate rate since it was more attractive than any plan they could get on their own. If employees went over the corporate plan for the number of minutes, they would be responsible for paying the difference. Each employee signed an agreement detailing the plan.

19A.3   PROBLEM 3—BILLING ISSUES

"Recently, my company purchased digital phones for our outside sales staff. These phones were intended to take the place of calling cards and reduce our phone expenses," writes one harried accounts payable professional on the discussion group. "Since we switched to digital phones four months ago, I have had nothing but problems with the billing." A few of the problems she noted were roaming charges (although she was told that the package included free roaming) and being billed for calls because, according to the carrier, they went over their allotted minutes.

The person reporting this incident says that when she received the bills with the roaming charges, she created an Excel spreadsheet to see how many employees went over. With a few minor exceptions, no one had. When she confronted the carrier, they responded that even though her company was on the one-rate, no roaming, no long-distance plan, roaming did occur when employees went outside their digital service area.

Because of this, the analog carrier for the outside area then billed the carrier. Complicating the issue even further, there were time delays in getting the roaming charges. These delays made it look like employees went over their allotment when actually they had not because they had not used all of the minutes from the previous month.

So what did she do? She tried explaining her side of the situation to the carrier. They were reluctant to believe her, but after looking at her carefully created spreadsheet, they had no choice. Her battle, however, was still not over. The cellular phone company's billing department would not issue credit. Each month, she must send the sales rep a copy of the spreadsheet and he manually adjusts the amount. This is a tremendous amount of additional work.

19A.4   PROBLEM 4—SALES AND USE TAX ON ROAMING

Those who are exempt from sales and use tax may have difficulty getting it removed from roaming charges. "I work for a public university," confides another weary accounts payable professional.

"We are tax exempt from sales and excise taxes on all telephone service, including cellular. When our users roam, they get hit with roaming charges that include sales taxes passed along from the roaming cell provider."

What does this savvy professional do? She doesn't pay them! She tells the phone company it should have thought of that when it agreed to take the university on as a customer. "The accounts receivable people hate us," she says, "but when they threaten to cut us off, I call their bluff. They have entirely too many accounts with my university and its regional campuses to cut any of us off." She does not think that this is an ideal solution, but she does not have a better one to offer. "Such an adversarial relationship is not a good idea for anyone, but the cellular industry is so competitive now that they're making all sorts of service contracts that are designed with an individual caller in mind, not a company," she concludes. This, of course, makes it difficult for the accounts payable professional left to deal with the mess.

Clearly, cell phones are here to stay. Companies are starting to accept the fact that they must establish a corporate-wide policy. Until that happens, accounts payable professionals will have to deal with the issue as best they can.

21

Internet and E-mail

p. 253. Insert at end of page:

21.3 INVOICES OVER THE INTERNET (NEW)

Are you ready to handle an infusion of invoices from your vendors over the Internet? Have you developed systems and procedures that will handle transactions being initiated not only on your company Web site, but also on someone else's? Think the Internet won't play such an intrusive role in business commerce for another five to ten years? Well, think again. Both General Motors and Ford have announced massive plans to become powerful entities in the e-commerce arena—and we are not talking about selling cars.

By the end of 2001, General Motors expects to make all of its $87 billion purchases through its Web site. Whether it's steel for a manufacturing plant or pencils for its executives, the orders will be placed over the Internet. Ford Motor Company has similar plans. That is not all. Both companies expect their suppliers to purchase and sell excess inventory through the GM or Ford Web site. Because General Motors has approximately 30,000 suppliers—only slightly more than Ford—this will prove to be a massive undertaking. Even if you do not do business with General Motors or Ford, you may very well buy from some of the same suppliers, who will have the ability to accept orders online in the new virtual marketplace.

(a) What Accounts Payable Pros Can Expect

Although Ford and GM may not meet their aggressive targets, they will come close. Once their suppliers have invested the money to go online as required, many will like it and in turn require that their suppliers go online as well. This will increase the number of companies participating in the automotive-based virtual marketplace. Other industries are sure to follow suit once the cost savings become apparent.

Most experts estimate that it costs approximately $100 for automotive companies to process a PO, but most of this processing cost can be saved using the Internet. This is just the beginning of the savings. Given corporate America's zeal to cut costs, many other companies will begin participating in or developing their own virtual marketplaces.

Accounts payable professionals will feel pressure from purchasing and management to become e-commerce proficient and to find ways to modify existing systems and procedures to work under the new paradigm. In theory, a commerce model with information passing between buyer and seller electronically should leave little room for human error. This *should* translate into fewer discrepancies as a result of pricing or other information errors.

On the plus side for accounts payable, the purchasing professionals using the new systems will also be responsible for inputting all information. Not only will they have to become e-commerce proficient, they will be monitored by their own companies to ensure that they do everything correctly. This may fill some of the black holes into which needed information sometimes falls.

(b) Action Steps

This is an area where accounts payable professionals can be the missionaries within their own organizations. By alerting management to the upcoming changes and recommending changes to accommodate electronic commerce within the accounts payable department, managers will be ready when electronic orders and invoices become the norm.

The accounts payable department will have to be staffed with professionals who are 100% computer and related technology literate. This means not only knowing how to use the Internet, but also having a thorough understanding of the programming languages that will become the standard. XML is already a leading candidate in that field. Those who are ready for the change and can adapt quickly will not only survive but thrive in the new electronic marketplace.

* 21.4 THE GE APPROACH TO ELECTRONIC INVOICE AND PAYMENT PROCESS (NEW)

Like many companies, General Electric (GE) recognized the inherent inefficiencies of its paper-based payment process. Unlike other companies, when GE decides to change something, its suppliers generally get in line and do what GE wants. Speaking at the National Association of Purchasing and Payables Professionals annual conference, GE's Global Product Manager David W. Hay explained the company's approach to electronic invoicing and payment process. While most attendees did not have the same clout to implement an electronic invoicing program, they learned many valuable lessons from the seminar.

(a) GE's Vision

Hay described GE's vision for the future, which could be quite exciting for its accounts payable department. For starters, GE believes its electronic invoice and payment process should be PO-driven, including Web-enabled invoice and invoiceless settlement processes. It would also like its process to include transactional transparency that highlights status and history. The company would like to use workflow approval for complex transactions and services, and needs its final system to be global, and have multicurrency capabilities. A virtual three-way match, real time, is the goal.

The company believes that now is the time to start to develop an electronic process. Currently, 70 percent of its invoices are manual. This severely taxes its capabilities, and the company wonders if it will be able to handle its forecasted 7 trillion transactions. Its manual processes are very inefficient, so the company sees the opportunity for huge cost savings.

(b) Savings Opportunities

The company identified several savings prospects that moving into an electronic environment would make possible. These include:

- *Lost discount.* Most of its suppliers offer a discount of 1 to 3 percent for prompt pay. Currently, the company loses 77 percent of these due to processing inefficiencies. The savings attributable to attaining all of the eligible discounts on the company's estimated $45 billion annual spend is huge.

- *Reduced customer service costs.* The company's buyers spend up to 20 percent of their time answering calls about payments. This is compounded by the fact that 70 percent of the calls that come to the accounts payable department are from internal buyers following up on payments to vendors. Clearly, this area is ripe for process improvements.

- *Elimination of the two- and three-way match.* The current manual process is time-consuming, which leads to payment delays and is costly considering the high mismatch rate.

(c) Getting Started

The company evaluated its invoices and discovered that 82 percent of them were for less than $2,500. It also discovered that: it took anywhere from 25 to 40 days to process an invoice; 26 percent of the invoices failed the match; and 77 percent of trade discounts were missed. Since the company offers 60-day terms with an early discount available at 15 days, its existing processes made it impossible to take the discount. (Now many reading this may be thinking that the vendor offers terms, *not* the buyer, and that is correct, *unless* the buyer in question is GE which tells its vendors what terms it will pay.)

The company analyzed its defects and discovered that paper accounted for most of its problems. It analyzed its top six invoice errors by document type and found that:

- Thirty-two percent (32%) were for account number errors.
- Twenty-one percent (21%) were for receiving errors.
- Eleven percent (11%) were related to the PO.
- Ten percent (10%) were due to missing approvals.
- Six percent (6%) were attributable to advice line and quantity errors.
- Six percent (6%) had incorrect remit to addresses.

Clearly, the key to solving the problem lay in eliminating paper.

By preparing a detailed financial analysis, the company estimated that it could save $240 million annually if it could get a handle on its payment process to enable it to qualify for all of its discounts. There would be additional productivity savings if it could streamline its processes, thereby reducing or eliminating all those calls to accounts payable—something that would automatically fall into place if its vendors were being paid on time!

(d) The Solution: Part 1

For starters, the company requires a PO for everything. It then employs a variety of electronic initiatives for handling the payment piece. As you might expect, the company uses a p-card for all transactions under $2,500. This method is especially efficient at GE since the company has its own credit card program.

GE uses Evaluated Receipt Settlement (ERS) for direct materials. This approach is also referred to as *pay-on-receipt* or *invoiceless processing*. The company has certain existing EDI relationships, which it continues to employ. Like most other professionals, Hay does not see the application disappearing, despite the fact that he sees it as a dinosaur.

Finally, the company expects to use a Web invoicing settlement application for approximately one-third of its invoices, which do not fall into one of the other categories.

While each of the techniques has advantages for GE, none is perfect. Hay reviewed the pros and cons of each and his analysis is contained at the end of this section. He shared with the audience an interesting tidbit: Did you know that in China, execution can be a punishment for VAT fraud?

(e) The Solution: Part 2

The company was looking to reduce its processing time so it could take advantage of discounts, while simultaneously reducing the costs associated with the payment inquiries made to accounts payable. While the payment alternatives just described will make a serious dent in the problem, they do not provide the total answer. Therefore, the company is also considering:

- E-invoicing
- Self-service invoice inquiry
- Web invoice submission
- Automatic PO to invoice match
- Web payment status

(f) Measuring Success

As might be expected, a company like GE will regularly check to see if it is meeting its goals. In the case of the new invoice match and pay process, Hay says the company measures the following:

- *Trade discounts achieved*. GE hopes to earn at least 70 percent of those available, and appears to be exceeding that goal.
- *Cycle time*. In order to earn the discounts, the company set a goal of an eight-day cycle. At the time of Hay's talk, that goal had yet to be achieved.

- *PO failure.* There was still a bit of work to be done in this area.
- *Invoices processed.* The company was right on target in this area.

Since the system had only recently been implemented, GE had achieved a remarkable amount, although it felt it had a few areas left for improvement. We think the company has done an impressive job.

According to Hay and GE, the following summarizes the pros and cons of p-cards, ERS, Web invoicing, and EDI:

	PROS	**CONS**
P-card	Pay directly from the PO No invoice or payment cost	No opportunity for discounting Lack of acceptance of Level 3 data
ERS	Eliminate the three-way match Gain discounts Drop shipments not picked up by system	Need clean and accurate receiving Tax issues in VAT
Web Invoicing	Automate A/P functions Gain discounts	Requires matching Integration issues
EDI	Large existing supplier base Generally accepted standard	Mapping integration costs Reaches only largest suppliers

21A

How Accounts Payable Departments Are Using the Internet in the New Millennium (New)

The Internet is radically changing the way accounts payable professionals are running their departments. How so? While only a small percentage had Internet access just a few years ago, today four out of five accounts payable professionals are using e-mail accounts payable departments to improve productivity. That is just the beginning. The techniques discussed in this chapter are not being used by just high-tech, leading-edge companies but by companies of all sizes and sophistication.

21A.1   USES

The Web sites cited in this article were all operational at the time this supplement went to print. However, in the fast-paced Internet world, some may not be available six months down the road. Readers can find similar sites by doing searches using terminology such as "accounts payable manuals," "accounts payable policy and procedures," and so on. With a little trial and error, the reader will be able to find sites similar to those listed should the sites mentioned no longer be available.

- *Use e-mail to correspond with others within the company and with vendors.* Accounts payable professionals routinely use e-mail within their firms to get approvals and for follow-up matters. Those who would like to get a free e-mail account for personal use (but not Internet access) can get one from companies such as yahoo.com, rocketmail.com, hotmail.com, and the like.

- *Get help with accounts payable–related issues.* Accounts payable professionals can get advice from their peers by posting a query on *www.ioma.com/discussion/boards.html.* Although IOMA does not guarantee a response, most postings are answered, some by as many as eight different people. Another place to ask a question is RECAP's "Ask the Expert." Most receive a response within 48 hours. Point your browser to *www.recapinc.com/ask_the_experts.htm.*

- *Looking for a policy and procedures manual?* Don't reinvent the wheel. Several universities have posted their manuals. While you won't necessarily want to copy their manuals word for word, they do provide a good starting point. Three such sites are *www.128.138.92.18/apmanual/tc.htm, www.db.-erau.edu:80/appm/procedure/2-3-1.html,* and *www.gwu.edu/-~finhome/ap/ap-1.htm.*

- *Use FAQs.* Reduce the number of phone calls coming into the accounts payable department by preparing an FAQ (frequently asked questions) sheet to give to company employees who ask the same questions over and over again. A sample to get you going can be found at *www.vcu.edu/procurement/apfaqs.htm.*

- *Provide information within the company through your own accounts payable newsletter.* Use the newsletter to address issues with employees. Take a look at one prepared by an accounts payable department. It can be seen at *www.met-washairports.com/Authority/Financial/apnew499.pdf.*

- *Use the Internet.* Provide information to your employees on the Internet. A site that does it well is *www.uiowa.edu/-~our/opmanual/#fin.*

- *Research.* Research specific information you might need to do a better job. Use quotes (" "), plus (+), and the word to limit your search to the items you really need. *www.askjeeves.com* permits the user to ask questions in simple English rather than use search terminology; while *www.dogpile.com* compiles the results from a number of other search engines. *www.altavista.com* is another good search engine that accounts payable professionals use. There are others. Use the one that you are most comfortable with.

- *Get p-card information.* Here are several useful sites:

  www.americanexpress.com/cpc/docs/index.html

  www.mastercard.com/ourcards.corporate/purchasingcard.html

  www.visa.com/pd/comm/purch/main.html

  www.purchase-card.com

  co.stanford.edu/payments/disbursements/creditcards/pcard/manual/index.html

  www.purchasecard.sarda.army.mil/

- *Fraud.* Accounts payable professionals can never know too much about fraud. Here are some sites with information that will help you protect a company's assets:

  Positive pay: *www.positivepay.com/*

  Phony invoice schemes: *www.bbb.org/library/ba-inv.html*

  Controller of the currency: *www.occ.treas.gov/chckfrd/contents.htm*

  Renowned fraud expert Frank Abagnale: *www.abagnale.com/*

- *Wondering whether to take the discount?* Do not bother with the complicated calculations yourself. Simply point your browser to *www.loderdrew.com/html/discount_analysis_calculator.html*.

- *Looking for a new employee?* If you want someone who is Internet savvy, place your listing on one of the many job sites, including *ioma.com/discussion/boards.html, www.monsterboard.com/,* and *careerpath.com.*

- *1099 Information.* Accounts payable professionals need specialized tax information, specifically about 1099s and sales and use tax. Check out the following:

  www.adp.com

  www.payroll-tax.com

  www.paychex.com

  www.salestaxinstitute.com/

- *VAT refunds.* Not all accounts payable folks handle VAT refunds, but those who do can get information from the following sites:

  www.vrc-vatrefund.com/index.html

  www.autovat.com/index.html

  www.meridianvat.com/

  www.bizednet.bris.ac.uk/virtual/economy/policy/tools/-vat/vatws.htm

- *Information about organizations.* Accounts payable professionals looking for information about professional organizations can check out the following:

  www.iappnet.org

  www.americanpayroll.org

  tmanet.org

  www.aipb.com

- *Teach* your staff about letters of credit by letting them use the tutorial at *www.avgtsg.com.*

- *Check payment status.* Let vendors check their payment status on the Internet instead of making phone calls to the accounts payable department. Intel is one company that has done this. Check *supplier.intel.com/* and *supplier.intel.com/dobusiness/ap/*. If you want to do the same but do not know where to start, there is a company that sells software that will help. Point your browser to *www.openinvoice.com/*.

The Internet is changing the accounts payable function. Are you ready?

21A.2   GETTING STARTED

The most successful accounts payable professionals, when it comes to the Internet, are those who just get on the Web and experiment. The software needed to create a Web site can be very inexpensive, if not free. Those interested in setting up a Web site can start by creating a personal one. Many sites give away a small amount of space for free. Create a site related to a personal interest or charitable organization or one that demonstrates your own abilities. Just do it.

If your company is not ready to go full speed ahead, it may be necessary to develop Internet skills on your own. This is a smart move because many companies demand Internet skills of those they hire. If you cannot get those skills in your present position, get them on your own.

21A.3   A SUCCESS STORY

The Internet is the ideal tool to help harried accounts payable professionals deal more effectively with the challenges they encounter. At the IOMA/IMI Accounts Payable conference in Pasadena, Intel's accounts payable controller, Jeff Lupinacci, explained to attendees how his department uses the Internet and offered guidelines on how payables managers could do it themselves.

Do not assume that this was some big fancy project that only an accounts payable department in a Fortune 500 company like Intel could pull off. Lupinacci did not use high-powered consultants but rather accounts payable staffers. The entire project cost under $10,000 and that was three years ago. Today, it might be less.

(a) Setting Objectives

The most important step in setting up an accounts payable Web site is to determine your objectives. What do you hope to accomplish with the site? Lupinacci determined that Intel needed better customer service both for his internal and external customers, and set out to solve the following problems with the Web site:

- *Reduce phone calls.* The department received a large number of phone calls from both employees and suppliers. To reduce this number, the company employed 15 people to handle these phone calls.
- *Educate client base.* A search was on for a better form of marketing and educating his client base as to accounts payable requirements.
- *Get feedback.* A method for continuous feedback from customers was needed.
- *Reduce costs.* A way to reduce high printing costs of accounts payable forms and an easy way to distribute them was needed.
- *Centralize access.* For pertinent information to be distributed to those who worked outside the accounts payable department, centralized access was needed.

(b) Identifying Resources and Content

Getting information technology (IT) resources allocated to any department can be a problem, but an accounts payable department wanting to build its own Web site would perhaps face more obstacles—especially three years ago when both internal and external sites were more novel. Undeterred, the folks at Intel charged ahead. Lupinacci was also lucky. The site for employees was ultimately put up on an intranet (a closed Internet site for company employees only). For this purpose, the company's local area network (LAN) was used to host the site. A 486 personal computer served as the Web server.

Lupinacci pulled together a team of three people who worked on this project for a four-month period. Getting Web content just right is extremely important. Intel spent two months identifying the right content for its accounts payable Web site. Content/process experts were used to validate the information.

(c)   Designing the Site

If it is not easy to find information on a site, many people will not use it. Recognizing this fact, Intel spent a good deal of time making sure the data was logically arranged. This meant creating a design "bible" before the programming began. It was critical that all information be clear. Lupinacci says that at Intel, roughly a month was spent getting the information arranged and making it logically navigable. He says that they went through many revisions and looks before agreeing on the current design.

To ensure that the site was easily navigable, the amount of animation and pictures was limited. The group identified the appropriate color palette and other visual branding. It was also decided what bells and whistles were needed. Finally, the visual identity created for accounts payable was used on all subsequent marketing efforts.

(d)   Pulling the Content Together

As the group reached the point where the content solidified, it began converting the files and graphics into formats used on the Web. They chose Anawave's Hotdog Pro and used very few graphics because of system demands. While graphics make a sight visually pleasing and entertaining, they also impede the speed at which the site loads.

The formatting was tough because sites can sometimes appear one way on one computer using one browser and another on a different computer. The group had to find a format that looked good on multiple configurations. It is important that those developing their own sites take this into consideration and test their new site on more than one computer. If possible, test its use on an IBM clone and an Apple and, of course, Microsoft Explorer as well as Netscape Navigator.

Keep in mind that from time to time it will be necessary to create new content. Make allowances for this and plan for it in your budget process. Also, allocate the staff time to take care of this chore.

(e) Testing the Site

Quality control is another issue. Lupinacci emphasizes the importance of proofreading the site. It is very easy for spelling errors to creep into the copy. It is also important to have hardware that can withstand the number of visitors you will have to the site. He recommends spending at least two weeks testing and checking the quality of the site; he strongly suggests not launching the site too early. Tell only a few loyal users and let them play around with it until you are sure the kinks have been worked out.

When Intel's accounts payable department first launched its Web site, access was limited within the department. Feedback was via survey and e-mail, with Lupinacci providing incentive for everyone to check it out. The test phase lasted three weeks, with more than 100 people providing input.

(f) Marketing Your Accounts Payable Home Page

You may think that once you have finally gotten your home page up and running, the battle is over. However, it has just begun. The first step is to make others aware of your Web site. Moving forward all business documents should have the Web address or universal resource locator (URL) on them. Intel had a mass-mailing to inform employees of the home page. This was sent not only through the internal mail but also via e-mail. In eight months, Lupinacci was able to establish a 79% awareness level within the company.

Posters were placed in the cafeterias announcing the site, and an article was published in the in-house IT publication. Organizations with company newsletters can have announcements carried there as well. At Intel, whenever an employee called the accounts payable department with a question that could have been answered if they had accessed the Web site, they were pointed in that direction.

Those who develop such a site need to recognize that they will never get 100% of potential users to surf for answers. Still, the thought of eliminating more than half the calls coming into accounts payable should provide enough incentive.

(g)   Maintenance

A good Web site must be updated frequently, says Lupinacci. He is not alone in this view. If it is not continually fed new information, visitors will not come back to see it again. He recommends continually checking for accuracy, especially if the organization is in a continuous improvement mode. As the company changes its accounts payable policies or procedures, the Web site will have to be updated to reflect these.

Many Web sites have a "What's New" section (or page) that is updated daily, weekly, or monthly—whatever is appropriate for the business. At Intel, the accounts payable "What's New" page is updated every two weeks.

Lupinacci suggests creating links with key business partners as they get their home pages up and running. He gives the example of Finance Information Systems, Purchasing, and Corporate Travel. The links you choose will depend on the nature of the business and whether other departments within the company have their own sites. He reviews the site monthly to ensure data accuracy.

Expect to receive e-mail requests from your Web page. At Intel, the customer service center was established as a mechanism to reply to e-mail. In addition, one full-time employee maintains and updates the accounts payable site. The amount of resources needed to allocate to the site depends on the complexity of the site and the amount of new data added.

He noted that it is important to monitor hardware. What is adequate today may not do the job a year or two down the road.

(h) Post-Implementation

With the site up and running, the amount of user feedback diminishes greatly, but not completely. There needs to be a "gate-keeper," someone responsible for a centralized review of the content, target audience, and placement of the material on the site. Responsibility for content must be assigned so that appropriate information is supplied for updates and improvements. Lupinacci recommends that content be reviewed quarterly and outdated material removed.

Once the site is out there, make sure that it is visited and the right visitors are visiting the right pages. No accounts payable site needs a bunch of teenagers peering through its contents. Hit counters are not enough, says Lupinacci. He wants to know who hits what pages and how long they stay there. This is the information he feels he needs to keep the site top notch.

He captures customer feedback via e-mail. He also surveys his customers annually and at point of service. As an added feature, he involves select customers to participate in usability testing.

Even this is not enough for Lupinacci. Although he benchmarks internally with other functional groups, he continually surfs the Net looking for ideas and standards. However, he says that it is still hard to find other accounts payable sites, although there are a few. He is right. Accounts payable is only starting to get the recognition it deserves and, with it, the resources to accomplish what Lupinacci has.

21A.4   WHAT SHOULD BE INCLUDED ON THE A/P WEB PAGE

An accounts payable Web site or page should be accessible via any company intranets as well as the Internet. By building on the experiences of their peers, accounts payable professionals will be able to construct the best possible payable Web sites for their companies.

(a)   Intranet

For intranet users, the A/P page should offer:

- Answers to frequently asked accounts payable questions
- Accounts payable contact list, with phone extensions and responsibilities
- Accounts payable deadlines for check requests
- Accounts payable policy and procedures manual
- T&E policy and forms
- Petty cash policy and forms
- Purchasing card information
- All other accounts payable forms
- Copies of past issues of your internal accounts payable newsletter, if you have one

(b)   Internet

For Internet users, the A/P site should include:

- Payment status of open invoices
- Accounts payable contact list, with phone numbers and responsibilities
- Company's invoice and supplier policies
- Company's W-9 policy for independent contractors

21A.5   ELECTRONIC INVOICING

A paperless office has long been the dream of innovative, forward-thinking accounts payable professionals. While this is not likely to happen in the near future, certain innovations are bringing this dream one step closer to reality. Imaging and workflow technology are the first giant step toward this fantasy. There is yet another innovation that could bring a paperless office within the reach of virtually every accounts payable department and make expensive imaging equipment obsolete in the process. We are talking about electronic invoicing. What follows is a review of the services offered by five of the companies currently offering electronic invoicing products. No two are identical. Each addresses some of the obstacles accounts payable professionals could run into when implementing electronic invoicing.

(a) What Is Electronic Invoicing?

This is the electronic delivery of invoices, mostly over the Internet, to the accounts payable department. No paper is received. The accounts payable department forwards, via e-mail, the invoice to the person who needs to approve it. The information is then available, without further keying, to be housed on a network for data retrieval purposes.

(b) Why Is Electronic Invoicing Attractive?

In addition to the elimination of mountains of paper, accounts payable professionals like electronic invoicing because of:

- Elimination of mistakes due to rekeyed information
- Fears about the mail
- Use of easy workflow to route invoices for approval
- Cost reduction
- Difficulty in blaming accounts payable for others' own shortcomings in processing paper

(c) Usage

So, if this is such a great deal, why aren't companies signing up en masse? We wondered about the same thing and asked the product sponsors. The obstacles include:

- Cost
- Implementation time
- Budget constraints

- Internal resistance to change
- Lack of ease of use
- Difficulty in signing up partners
- Fear

(d)   Overcoming the Obstacles

Accounts payable professionals who can determine the reason their companies are holding back are in the best position to offer counterarguments for making electronic invoicing the right choice.

If budget constraints and/or cost are issues, iPayables' Kim Rawlings suggests presenting "compelling ROI (return on investment) data to build the business case for the initiative." She is happy to help accounts payable professionals interested in her product to make their case. BillingZone recommends the same approach. Its representatives point out that Electronic Invoice Presentment and Payment (EIPP) offers both billers and payers a significant value proposition by eliminating paper from the process. BillingZone says that improved customer service, cash management, and accuracy in tracking and taking discounts are added benefits that can be factored into the equation.

Those facing the anonymous complaints of "it will take too long" or "our vendors won't use it" should rely on documentation supplied by the service provider. "We lay out a well-defined process and work with clients to ensure that the project is managed," says Open Business Exchange's Martha Perlin. Many of these vague complaints vanish when the parties understand what is expected of them and how the electronic invoicing process will work.

Fear of the unknown is a concept many accounts payable professionals have encountered when trying to implement a new process. It is also what many are finding when they mention electronic invoicing in their own shops. "Validating the concept is probably the lengthiest process involved to garner buy-in from companies as a whole," points out Direct Commerce's Lisa Sconyers. "The result of such an application offers big money savings opportunities as well as extreme process streamlining, but our current economic market has instilled fear and conservatism toward implementing new technology," she concludes.

Sconyers has a few recommendations for accounts payable professionals who face this dilemma. She suggests calling and getting referrals from customers already using the product. She points out that since her company can quickly and efficiently configure and integrate its application in a matter of days, a pilot program will give potential clients the opportunity to test the product firsthand without any risk.

Xign's Chris Rauen recommends that the accounts payable professional search for a solution that accommodates the buy-side processing needs, simplifies supplier enrollment and ramp-up, and provides material benefits to both trading parties.

(e) Selecting the Best Service

The five companies interviewed about electronic invoicing provided the information in Section (f). As is readily observable, each of the products has distinct advantages and works differently. Each company interested in pursuing the e-invoicing route will base its own decision on its:

- Existing internal processes
- Budget
- Corporate culture
- Willingness to mandate changes both internally and externally

Check out the Web sites and/or contact those vendors whose products interest you. Although e-invoicing may seem like a leading-edge approach today, in just a few short years it will be commonplace. Remember when p-cards were considered innovative?

(f) Overview of Existing Electronic Invoicing Services

The information below was provided by each of the companies that offers e-invoicing services.

Name: InvoiceWorks™ and ClearGear™

Company: iPayables

Description: By allowing vendors to key or upload invoice information via the Internet, iPayables eliminates paper from the invoicing process. iPayables makes it possible for invoice payers to receive invoices electronically from all vendors and suppliers regardless of their size or technical ability. The InvoiceWorks™ and ClearGear™ applications allow easy routing, approval, and delivery of invoices from vendors and suppliers to payer's accounts payable systems.

Cost: Initial setup and implementation cost less than $100,000. Per-invoice transaction fee is $1.45 or lower, depending on invoice volume. Annual maintenance is $15,000. All expenses are paid by clients. Vendors/suppliers are not charged for using service.

Advantages:

- Reduce invoice-processing cost by 70% to 90%
- Strengthen vendor relationships
- Eliminate data entry
- Reduce processing time from days and weeks to minutes
- Provide detailed history and audit trail
- Eliminate lost invoices
- Reduce clerical staff by 30% to 50% and reassign existing staff
- Keep labor costs under control
- Reduce vendor inquiry calls dramatically through online tracking and status
- Capture more negotiated term discounts
- Eliminate keying errors
- Reduce discrepancies, costs, and processing time

Web site: *www.ipayables.com*

E-mail: *kim.rawlings@ipayables.com*

Phone: 877-774-7932

Name: BillingZone.com™

Company: BillingZone

Description: BillingZone.com's EIPP service facilitates B2B transactions between billers and their payers. BillingZone.com is a simple way to present and pay invoices online and make the management of complex workflow issues such as invoice routing easy. Payers receive invoices from multiple billers on a single Web site to review, schedule, dispute, and pay invoices.

Cost: BillingZone's fee structure is based on a one-time implementation fee and transaction fees. BillingZone offers solutions to both billers and payers with fees based on the complexity of the implementation and the invoices themselves. The typical implementation fee is less than $100,000. BillingZone has implemented many companies for less than this amount.

Advantages:

- Consolidated solution for billers and payers
- Service is not software
- Bank neutral, not requiring any banking changes
- Payer focused

Web site: *www.billingzone.com*

E-mail: *info@billingzone.com*

Phone: 877-965-4583

Name: Direct Invoicing

Company: Direct Commerce

Description: Direct Commerce Invoicing (DCI) automates manual, tedious, and error-prone processes between the accounts payable department and their vendors. They provide services to:

- Accept electronic invoices
- Deliver purchase orders
- Validate documents according to business rules and purchase order information

- Translate between different formats
- Allow vendors to perform inquiries
- Notify vendors of payments and other invoice status changes
- Facilitate dialog and dispute resolution
- Route invoices for encoding and approval within organizations

Cost: Though both buyers and their vendors derive significant benefits from the Direct Commerce services, the fees are paid by the buying organization because they are the recipients of the tremendous cost savings. The pricing is based on a transaction fee, which typically falls into the range of $2 per invoice.

Advantages: DCI offers more than just the electronic delivery of invoices and POs. They actually manage the functionality and translate the information of the documentation within the processing of the invoice and PO (i.e., workflow, matching, data validation, approval escalation). This allows for two-way, straight-through processing and accurate information translation between two organizations.

Web site: *www.directcommerce.com*

Contact: Lisa Sconyers

E-mail: *lsconyers@directcommerce.com*

Phone: 415-288-9701

Name: OB10

Company: Open Business Exchange

Description: OB10 is a secure system that facilitates the delivery of invoices between trading partners. Each buyer and its vendors can choose the most appropriate data format, standard, and means of communication. Using sophisticated data-mapping technology, OB10 transforms and delivers all invoices from any vendor to any buyer.

Cost:

For buyer:

- Set-up fee $20,000 per accounting system/ERP
- Annual subscription $10,000

- Volume-based pricing per invoice averages 25¢ to 75¢, depending on volume
- Charges for optional services by invoice or unit

For vendor with accounting system:

- No set-up fee
- Annual subscription $750
- Volume-based pricing averages 25¢ to $1.00, depending on volume
- Charges for optional services by invoice or unit
- For vendor with no accounting system/using OBE's Web-based invoice creation and delivery:
  - Annual flat fee depends on volume, with a maximum of $100 per year
  - No charge for vendors with 12 or fewer invoices per year

Advantages:

- Buyer-driven solution
- No software or hardware installation
- Independent of formats or standards
- Short implementation time frames
- Quick ROI
- Benefits to vendors as well as buyers
- Solution accommodates all vendor types
- Secure data storage
- Full audit trail available to reduce disputes and expedite resolution

Web site: *www.obexchange.com*

E-mail: *martha.perlin@obexchange.com*

Phone: 212-828-2147

Name: Xign Disburser

Company: The Xign Payment Services Network (XPSN)

Description: Buyers configure settings and rules for optimal processing of electronic invoices, including automation of data validation, posting, prioritization, routing, and approval (subject to buyer rules). Both parties track status online from submission through receipt of payment.

Cost: Both buyers and suppliers pay fees for the services delivered to them. Pricing varies in proportion to the client's transaction volumes and to the benefit delivered. Buyers pay an annual subscription fee based on usage volumes. Suppliers pay a modest registration fee. Transaction charges are based on a percentage of savings from electronic processing.

Advantages:

- Buy-side electronic invoice aggregation
- Few exceptions
- Automated posting, approval, prioritization, and routing
- Accelerated dispute notification and resolution
- Online settlement status tracking
- Precise control over settlement timing
- Accurate cash flow forecasting
- Efficient use of working capital
- Supplier directory data maintained by suppliers
- Complete online audit trail
- Simple to implement

Web site: *www.xign.com*

E-mail: *info@xign.com*

* 21A.6 THE INTERNET: A/P PROS FIND NUMEROUS USES FOR THE INTERNET IN EVERYDAY A/P FUNCTIONS

What is the number-one reason why accounts payable managers are using the Internet? Respondents of the *Managing Accounts Payable 2002 Benchmarking Survey* say they are using the Internet for invoices—to receive them electronically and then to forward them to the appropriate personnel for approvals. This is further evidence that e-invoicing is starting to take hold in corporate America. The survey also revealed several other interesting insights, which lead us to conclude that accounts payable is rapidly changing from a clerical manual function to one that requires research, analysis, and a thorough understanding of the business process.

(a) The Data

Virtually every accounts payable professional with Internet access at work uses e-mail. Previous studies have shown that in excess of 90 percent of accounts payable professionals have and use e-mail at work. Thus e-mail usage is a given. But we wanted to know if and how accounts payable professionals were using the Internet. Over one-quarter of the survey respondents shared with us significant ways they were using the Internet:

- Overall, just fewer than 30 percent of those making significant use of the Internet did so with regard to invoices. They either received invoices electronically or went to vendors' sites to pick up their invoices.
- Almost an equal number of accounts payable professionals reported using the Internet for various types of research purposes. This proves that accounts payable professionals are starting to play a significant role within their organizations.

(b) Invoices

Companies are receiving invoices and going to vendors' sites to pick them up. Some are using third-party systems, while others are simply taking in the invoices attached to an e-mail. A few others are expanding the practice. Here are a few examples:

- Use FTP to receive parts freight vendor invoices.
- Receive invoice data in text files from a container lease company. Each invoice, in this example, contains 2 to 1,000 records.
- Have vendor enter invoice information on customers' Web sites.

(c) Research

Anyone who thinks that accounts payable associates do nothing but process paper will be in for a shock when they see some of the tasks being researched on the Internet by today's professionals. Here are a few of the samples:

- Confirm correct addresses.
- Check UPS and FedEx tracking codes.
- Verify zip codes.
- View Bill of Lading (BOL) and signed receipts through freight company sites.
- Verify tax information.
- Verify currency conversion rates.
- Check vendors' sites for tracking information.
- Research regulatory information.
- Report independent contractors to the state.
- Look up the licenses and status of subcontractors.
- Research property tax bills.
- Verify new vendors.
- Check air rates, car rental rates, and hotels.
- Obtain signed proofs of delivery.
- Check vendor sites for statements and past-due invoices, where available.

- Use information to present new procedures and ideas.
- Find additional information about suppliers.
- Locate 1099 information and company card account/ transactions.
- Find floor plan financing information.
- Research outstanding balance issues with vendors.

(d)   Communicate with Suppliers

Any accounts payable professional who has played telephone tag with a vendor, or listened to a long drawn-out mumbled telephone message (and who hasn't?) appreciates the convenience of "talking" with suppliers via e-mail. Accounts payable professionals are taking advantage of this benefit of e-mail and using it effectively for dispute resolution, to follow up on invoice status, and obtain vendor information that may not be included on the invoice.

Some are also using e-mail to request copies of lost or missing invoices; and internally, to obtain branch approvals, verify receipt of goods, and respond to credit inquiries.

(e)   Banking

When corresponding with their banks, accounts payable professionals have found a dozen ways to use the Internet. They include

- Putting a stop payment on a check
- Processing bank transfers
- Looking up checks
- Making payroll tax payments
- Banking online
- Conducting wire transfers
- Making direct deposit
- Executing currency exchanges
- Sending file transfers to the bank

- Paying federal taxes
- Viewing bank statements
- Using positive pay

(f) Other

P-cards are a natural for the Internet, and many accounts payable professionals verify their billings and pull reports directly from the Internet. While some regularly download p-card and T&E information, others take the downloaded T&E information and upload it directly into the employees' expense reports.

What is obvious is that the Internet is playing an important role in the everyday life of accounts payable professionals everywhere.

* 21A.7 CASE STUDY: EXPERT DEMONSTRATES HOW TO PUT THE WEB TO WORK FOR ACCOUNTS PAYABLE

We've all heard the expression, "don't work harder, work smarter." Companies everywhere are starting to implement that approach by taking advantage of the Internet to control areas such as invoice handling, T&E, and procurement. Speaking at Recap's Enhancing Accounts Payable conference, Charles Schwab's Vice President Sandy Campos explained how her company harnessed the power of the Web to achieve these goals.

(a) Background

"Just when you think you understand the game," began Campos, "somebody changes the rules." That's certainly the way it's been in accounts payable at Schwab over the last few years. She said that Schwab experienced tremendous growth in the last five years of the 1990s. The firm's operational and administrative functions struggled to keep pace with the growth, utilizing the obvious strategy: It hired more people to handle the ever-growing transaction volume. Then, one day, a light went on. The firm realized that just hiring more people was not an effective long-term prescription to address the corporate growing pains.

Schwab needed to free up people to focus on the core business. Campos says that the way the company is doing this is by creating a self-service environment, which offers streamlined, paperless, seamless, online access to information. While this sounds wonderful in theory, how can accounts payable departments achieve this goal?

(b) Getting Started

It wasn't difficult to identify the processes that were ripe for improvement. Campos says the company decided to focus on processes that were: in support of employee and third-party self-service, manually intensive, and repetitious in nature. Processes that were also ripe for improvement were those that were challenging to control, time-consuming, managed by several organizations, paper-based, and geographically dispersed.

With so many areas fitting these descriptions, the difficult part was to identify those accounts payable functions that did *not* meet the criteria.

(c) Goals

In accounts payable, Schwab wanted to achieve three specific goals:

1. *Cycle time.* The company wanted faster processing, the elimination of duplicate data entry, and the reduction of errors. Additionally, it wanted online update and edit capabilities and workflow.

2. *Information availability.* Ideally, the company strove to have real-time access to current information, to reduce printing and distribution costs and to eliminate paper.

3. *Process controls.* The company wanted to enforce requirements and standards and to automate the audit process by applying defined business rules and policies.

(d)   What Schwab Has Accomplished

The company implemented a number of electronic initiatives, including:

- *Invoice handling.* Invoices are scanned to create a digital image, which is electronically routed to cost center managers for online review and approval of the expenditure. This replaces a manual paper-intensive process whereby invoices were received in accounts payable, copied, and then sent via internal mail for review and approval by the appropriate cost center manager.
- *eT&E.* Replacing the paper reimbursement forms that had to be completed and mailed to accounts payable for manual data input and payment processing was an e-mail-based T&E application (eT&E). It is routed electronically for approval, processing, and payment. Reimbursement now occurs in two to three days instead of two to three weeks.
- *eTimesheets.* Paper timesheets that were mailed or faxed to payroll twice a month have been replaced with a Web application. Employees record their hours electronically twice a month.
- *Travel planner.* Instead of calling a corporate travel office to coordinate reservations for business travel arrangements, most travel plans can be made by accessing an internal Web site and reserving airline tickets, hotel rooms, and rental cars.
- *Employee 401K and stock option statements viewable via an intranet.* Formerly, these were printed and mailed quarterly.
- *Ariba procurement.* Employees log in to the Web-based Ariba application to place orders through online catalogs. These orders are automatically routed to preferred vendors. This system replaces a paper-based system that required approvals and was mailed to purchasing for creation of a PO and sourcing.

- *Financial reporting.* Managers with access to FIN!Web have real-time access to revenue and expense data for their assigned cost centers, and have the ability to electronically record accruals and reclasses. This replaces a system from which analysts ran endless reports each month for e-mail distribution to appropriate managers for review.

The last item shows just how much the game has changed. When the e-mail distribution methodology was introduced, it was considered a big improvement over the old system, from which reports were printed and distributed to the appropriate managers. And indeed it was a major improvement over the old; but, as this example demonstrates, just as quickly as something becomes a best practice, it becomes commonplace or standard and, eventually, obsolete.

Those who know Campos realize that she is not one to rest on her laurels or accomplishments. She has goals for the future—plans to take Schwab further down the information superhighway, and she shared some of those future enhancements. Specifically, she is looking at:

- Web-based payments
- Electronic invoicing
- Electronic pay stubs
- eAction forms
- Web benefits enrollment

Clearly, Campos is a big fan of Web-based technologies. In closing her remarks at the conference, she noted, "There are countless opportunities for your company to improve both internal operating efficiency and the bottom line by putting the Web to work for you." Savvy accounts payable professionals will follow her advice.

21B

Encryption and Digital Signatures (New)

21B.1 INTRODUCTION

For good reason, some professionals are concerned about the lack of security when using the Internet. One company that has made great strides in using the Internet and incorporating state-of-the-art security is Chevron. The solution to the security problem lies in encryption and digital signatures. A/P professionals need to understand that these new technologies are coming to accounts payable—quickly.

21B.2 BASICS

At several recent conferences, Chevron's manager of accounts payable reengineering, James M. Burstedt, and Ed Ames, a Chevron analyst for electronic commerce and a cofounder of the Unclaimed Property Holders Association, explained these approaches, and how they are reflected by Chevron's corporate policy.

(a) Corporate Policy

The Chevron policy states, "Information and the systems supporting it are key company assets, requiring prudent and proactive protection by information owners and users alike. It is the policy of the company to secure these assets from external and internal threats through a combination of technology, practices, processes and monitoring, based on risk and the value of the assets. The goal is to minimize the potential for damage, either purposeful or accidental, to the company's computer and communications systems, company data and information." This policy allows Chevron to focus its resources to protect its most important asset: its information. Like other companies, Chevron needs to protect itself from hackers, pranksters, dishonest insiders, competitors, and information terrorists. It is concerned about viruses, interception, prying eyes, alteration or loss of data, communication blocks, and system disruptions. However, the biggest concern is unauthorized access.

(b)   The Origins of the Problem and Some Solutions

Burstedt and Ames pointed out that security breaches can occur: an intruder masquerading as an employee; eavesdropping; data being changed en route; e-mail addresses being changed en route; or passwords and identifications being cracked or stolen. The speakers also identified the defenses that stop unauthorized access to computer information transferred over the Internet. These include authentication (digital signature and private key/hash), encryption, digital certificates (ID validation/nonrepudiation), firewalls, and strong passwords.

 The consequences of not having these defenses can be severe. Financial loss, damage to the company's reputation, loss of business, legal actions, and the loss of strategic information are only a few of the possible results.

 When an employee's laptop is stolen, the biggest loss is not the cost of the laptop, but the strategic information stored on the hard drive. Thus, Chevron relies on what it calls "secured messaging."

(c)   Secured Messaging

Chevron defines *secured messaging* as the use of encryption and digital signatures. Before defining what a digital signature is, let us focus on what it is not. It is *not* a digitized signature, the manual signature by an individual on an electronic device such as those used by certain department stores for charge card purchases. Burstedt and Ames provided the following definitions:

- *Digital signature.* Unique to a person and using a private key, digital signatures can be verified as belonging specifically to and used solely by that person. A digital signature is linked to data, so any change to the data will invalidate the signature. It is also nonrefutable, which means that a person can prove he or she sent a communication and, conversely, cannot deny that he or she sent it. It is the equivalent to getting a document notarized in the paper world.

- *Encryption* is the ability to transform electronic information into an unreadable format that can be converted back to its original readable state only by specific individuals previously authorized to do so.

- *Encryption engines,* also known as encryption algorithms, are now powerful enough to generate truly random keys, taking this responsibility out of the hands of people. It also allows for session keys that can be used once or multiple times and then discarded.

(d) Back to Math Class

Upon hearing the word *algorithm,* some of the accounts payable professionals reading this may vaguely remember high school math class. An *algorithm* is a detailed sequence of calculations performed in a specific number of steps to achieve a desired outcome.

A *hash algorithm* is a function that reduces a message to a mathematical expression; it is called a one-way hash because the expression cannot be reversed. For example, if every letter of the alphabet were assigned a number (a = 1, b = 2, etc.), any name could be reduced to a single digit. The speakers chose Julius Caesar because he was one of the earliest users of encryption.

J	U	L	I	U	S		C	A	E	S	A	R
10	21	12	9	21	19		3	1	5	19	1	18

$$\text{The sum for Julius} = 92, \qquad \text{The sum for Caesar} = 47$$
$$9 + 2 = 11 \qquad\qquad\qquad 4 + 7 = 11$$
$$11 + 11 = 22$$
$$2 + 2 = 4$$

Therefore, the hash total for Julius Caesar is 4.

Altering any original message or file, including changing the spelling of a word, eliminating apostrophes, or changing a comma to a period, will result in a different hash.

(e) PKI

Messages are encrypted and decrypted using public and private keys. Expect to hear much more about public key infrastructure (PKI) in the upcoming months as commerce continues to move to the Internet. The Chevron speakers also offered a clear explanation of how these keys are used:

> Two sets of electronic keys are used to encrypt and decrypt documents. Public keys can be shared while private keys are known only to their specific owner. An encrypted document is created using the sender's private key and the receiver's public key. The receiver decrypts the document using the sender's public key and the receiver's private key. The public key is the certificate authority. Separate pairs of keys can be used to encrypt or digitally sign to strengthen security. . . .
>
> Whatever is locked by a private key can only be unlocked by the corresponding public key and vice versa. Encrypting and sending with the sender's private key and the receiver's public key can therefore only be decrypted with the receiver's private key and the sender's public key. Use the private key to create the digital signature/hash.

Readers should be aware that currently there is a huge debate over setting standards for the PKI. It does not look like the question will be settled soon, as a number of entities have a vested interest in becoming the standard setter. These concepts may be new to many reading this, but it is imperative that anyone who works for a company that uses the Internet understand these concepts. Remember, there was a time, not too long ago, when the whole idea of the Internet seemed alien.

21B.3 CASE STUDY

Are you sure that every check and wire request you receive is valid? Are you concerned that perhaps some of those requisitions for large-dollar payments from overseas may not be from legitimate sources? Do you want to verify that the money you send out goes where it is supposed to go? Does using the Internet for data transmission make you uncomfortable? Well, the accounts payable folks at Chevron also had these concerns, but they were especially concerned about requests for payments coming from overseas. Although the project started with accounts payable, the hope was that it would be broad enough eventually to encompass other applications in all departments.

(a) Project Scope

Chevron had three main objectives for the technology solution it devised: *employ* commercial software to support encryption needs throughout the company; *install* software that would initially be used to encrypt e-mail and documents for storage and distribution; and *develop* an application for the payment request process using encryption and digital signatures.

Chevron felt that it was important to use encryption to:

- Protect data from unauthorized access
- Transport confidential data via the Internet
- Have digital signatures for the authorization of transactions such as payment requests
- Ensure that the person who sent the encrypted note was the author, and also to provide confirmation of receipt

- Prevent exposure of confidential data when laptops are lost or stolen
- Select an industry leader as a software provider to increase the chances of interoperability

Although many people within Chevron already used encryption with e-mail, it was the goal of this project to include those submitting payment requests and the international sales staff in that group.

(b) Accounts Payable Business Drivers

Chevron started its project with a pilot application. Although both evaluated receipt settlement (ERS) and electronic data interchange (EDI) are used extensively, the accounts payable department still receives 11,604 manual payment requests annually. Of those transactions:

- 35% were for less than $1,000
- 10% were for amounts between $1,000 and $5,000
- 55% were for amounts over $5,000; these represented 99% of the dollars

Certain financial transactions were being authenticated with manual keys, but the company did not feel that the manual process sufficiently protected the company against potential theft. Chevron also felt that confidential data was not adequately protected. Finally the company's information protection compliance policy required higher levels of protection, such as encryption.

(c) The Pilot Application

The participants in the pilot study had very definite ideas about what they wanted. However, what they wanted and what was available were not quite the same. The pilot program had a number of objectives, many of which were technical and were intended to set the groundwork so the program could be expanded after the accounts payable portion had been successfully implemented. Specific goals for accounts payable included:

- Creating an automated payment request form incorporating digital signatures
- Marketing the electronic form to company personnel
- Linking the payment request form to encryption (digital signatures and validation)
- Addressing the legal implications of digital signatures and human resources issues of inappropriate use

(d)   Developing an Electronic Form

The accounts payable department now had the opportunity to reengineer its existing practices through the development of an automated payment request form. Specifically, it:

- Replaced all existing payment request forms
- Made blank forms available through the company intranet, eliminating the need to print and store forms
- Included all pertinent fields for both domestic and international payments
- Included a pop-up window with help information for each field
- Employed encryption software for digital signature functionality
- Required multiple digital signatures for preparation and various approvals
- Prevented unauthorized changes due to the digital signature lock-down feature
- Allowed for the verification of each digital signature against the certificate authority file
- Included instructions for completion of the form and processing steps

(e) A Few Thoughts about Passwords

The advice the speakers gave regarding the use of passwords is applicable to everyone, not just those implementing a high-tech system. Chevron advocates the use of robust passwords, those that include both upper- and lower-case letters and alphabetic and nonalphabetic characters. In addition, the message was sent that sharing passwords was forbidden.

(f) Pilot Survey and Results

To make sure they were on track and to uncover any unforeseen problems, the team at Chevron conducted a pilot survey. They asked about the:

- Enrollment form and process
- Downloading and configuring of encryption software
- Downloading and configuring of electronic form software
- General instructions
- Ease of using encryption and electronic forms
- Technical support
- Results and recommendations

They were pleased to find that user satisfaction was very high. However, they discovered that users wanted a hard copy of the documentation rather than being pointed to the Internet for instructions. They were also able to identify who should be using encryption, based on customer feedback.

The speakers pointed out that use of technology allowed them to reengineer the accounts payable processes. They see the accounts payable function evolving into one that is more analytical. Burstedt and Ames have shown what the future of accounts payable can be for those who grab the technology ball and run with it.

21C

E-Marketplaces and XML (New)

21C.1 INTRODUCTION

Technology continues to rapidly invade accounts payable operations and change the way the function is handled at companies of all sizes. Two of the latest breakthroughs, e-marketplaces and XML, are already having an impact on many accounts payable departments. To clarify how these will alter the payment process, we turned to Harris Bank's Hamish Forrest and Covansys' Terri Hinder, who spoke at length on the subject at the IOMA/IMI Advanced Accounts Payable Institute.

21C.2 E-MARKETPLACE

E-marketplaces or exchanges are rapidly changing the way business is conducted. Probably the best known is Covisint, for the automotive industry, described on its Web site (*www.covisint.com*) as: "a global, independent e-business exchange providing the automotive industry with leading collaborative product development, procurement and supply chain tools that give its customers the ability to reduce costs and bring efficiencies to their business operations."

Other exchanges include:

- Paper industry: *www.paperfiber.com/exchange/*
- Steel industry: *www.gsx.com/home_page.html*
- Coal industry: *www.thinkenergy.com*
- Aerospace industry: *www.exostar.com*

It should be noted that most exchanges, at least at this point, are not nearly as developed as the one put together by the automotive industry.

(a) Types of E-Marketplaces

In addition to being for industry or for all comers, e-marketplaces can be categorized by additional groupings. These include:

- Open marketplaces that are usually for MRO or indirect goods.
- Closed or private marketplaces that are typically part of a select industry and usually for direct goods.
- Horizontal or vertical and these can be open or closed.
- Auction and reverse auction. Reverse (or downward) auctions have the ability to drive costs down dramatically.

Recently, Emerson Electric faced the challenge of consolidating millions of dollars of printed circuit board purchases across 14 global divisions. The company used *freemarkets.com*, the market leader, at least to this point, for the auction-type exchanges. It purchased goods that historically would have cost it $36.1 million. It had 43 ISO 9000-certified suppliers. The downward auction resulted in 755 bids being placed. The company introduced several new qualified suppliers and consolidated its supply base from 58 to 9, saving $10 million in the process. Emerson is not alone; John Deere recently signed on with *freemarkets.com*.

(b)   Why Does A/P Care?

For starters, with the kind of savings mentioned above, corporate America is bound to take notice and flock to these sites in droves. Forrest says that because an e-marketplace is one of the ways in which companies are changing the way they do business with their trading partners, everyone will be affected. Ultimately, he warns, the payment mechanism will change.

E-marketplaces provide a better return for companies because the savings go right to the bottom line. Companies realize savings that can be attributable to both better pricing and process improvements, with better pricing accounting for only 20% of the savings.

E-marketplaces also help control maverick purchasing while providing new sales channels and industry information. They also help automate the payment process, ultimately replacing checks with Automated Clearing House (ACH) payments.

(c)   What Does This Mean for A/P?

Finally, companies are focusing on the long-ignored payment function. More than one exchange has fallen apart because no one focused on this aspect. Despite the Internet, 80% of all B2B payments are currently being made by check. Companies are trying to squeeze all possible cost savings out of the procure-to-pay cycle, however, and are now focusing on the payment process. One of the innovative ways they are doing this is through the use of payment engines.

Payment engines are electronic triggers for payment. They initiate the optimal payment vehicle based on rules you input. A simple example might be that an electronic shipping notice would trigger a payment thirty days after the date on the shipping notice. Forrest lists a few including:

- *Financialsettlementmatrix.com*
- *Clareon.net*
- *Surepay.com*

With their expertise in the payment process, Forrest says that it is only natural that banks be involved in the payment process in a trusted third-party role.

21C.3 XML

Hinder provides a new definition for XML. She calls it the glue that pulls e-commerce together. She claims that all you need to understand about XML is that it is formatted as tag-data-tag.

Here is an example of a well-formed XML document: <greeting type = "friendly">Hello, world!</greeting>. While you may not understand all the formatting that goes along with the sample, you certainly can understand the intent of the message.

Additionally, Hinder says that:

- Legal XML documents are called well formed.
- A well-formed document describes a logical tree.
- If a well-formed document conforms to an optional set of constraints (called a DTD), it is also valid.

But this is more than you really need to know about XML.

21C.4 XML AND STANDARDS

One of the most frequent complaints heard about XML is that there is more than one kind of XML. That is only partially true. Currently there are a few different XMLs, but they are all coming together as the different groups continue to work together. Hinder believes that in five years there will be a standard. Accounts payable professionals, however, cannot wait that long to get involved.

The emerging leader is something referred to as ebXML (electronic business extensible markup language), which was created in November 1999 as a result of a NATO meeting. Its charter, says Hinder, was to provide an open XML-language-based infrastructure enabling the global use of electronic business information in an interoperable, secure, and consistent manner by all parties in an 18-month period.

Not only did this group meet its goals, but the major players in all current e-commerce initiatives have agreed to follow ebXML as their end state e-commerce standard.

(a)   A/P's Role in Setting This Standard

Although they may not realize it, a number of the people reading this had a say in getting this standard set. Everyone who responded to the *Electronic Invoicing and Electronic Payment Information Task Force* survey (for the creation of a *standard* invoice) had their "vote" counted.

The results of that survey were used to create the Rapid e-Invoice, which was ultimately presented to the ANSI X12 committee as the "standard" for invoices. The Rapid e-Invoice is now available for use by anyone who wishes to use it. The form, along with much other related useful information, can be accessed through the Internet at *www.sandia.gov/elecinvoice/home.html.*

21C.5   WHAT SHOULD A/P DO TO GET READY?

For starters, learn as much as you can about e-commerce, XML, and the new payment initiatives. Visit the Web sites mentioned in Section 21C.2 as well as *ebXML.org* to learn as much as you can. At this point, there are only a few experts on these topics so with a little effort you can become one of those "in the know."

Find out if there is an exchange for your industry. You can do this by talking with the purchasing manager or doing a search on the Internet. Simply go to *www.google.com* or one of the other search engines and put in your industry and the word exchange (i.e., paper + exchange).

Get involved. Find out what your company is doing. Many companies are already working on e-commerce initiatives, and a few even think to get their accounts payable managers involved.

Section 21C.6 contains some additional advice for accounts payable professionals who want to become involved in the e-commerce team for their companies.

Closing Thoughts

Don't be surprised if you are rebuffed when you approach purchasing about its participation in e-marketplaces. While these portals are magnificent for reducing cost and improving purchasing efficiency, they can also significantly reduce the number of people needed to handle a company's procurement needs. Thus, many in purchasing do not necessarily see exchanges as a good thing.

To be completely honest about the matter, these exchanges, if adopted wholeheartedly, will ultimately have the same effect on the accounts payable staff. With fewer invoices coming to a company, many will be able to reduce accounts payable staffs. This does not mean, however, that accounts payable professionals should fight the use of e-marketplaces. That would simply be a waste of time and effort. "Don't go kicking and screaming," warns Hinder. You can lead the charge or be left behind—the decision is yours.

Accounts payable professionals who understand what is happening and take every opportunity to learn about these changes and become part of them are well on their way to being part of the management team at their companies in the twenty-first century. Where do you stand?

21C.6   HOW TO BECOME PART OF THE E-COMMERCE REVOLUTION

Although many accounts payable professionals would like to take part in the e-commerce changes, they don't know where to start. What follows is a list of things, based on some excellent advice from Hinder, that they can do so they don't get left behind as e-commerce takes off in their organizations.

1. Take an active role in your company's e-commerce initiatives.
2. Pursue being on the team in your industry's B2B exchange.
3. Research the cost of becoming a buyer on the B2B portals. This is not free; most of the exchanges are supported through transaction fees.

4. Work closely with industry associations.

5. Actively pursue the procurement e-commerce directions, keeping short-term solutions as flexible as possible to be open to change standards as they become available.

6. Take advantage of any of the free e-commerce offerings available from your customers and suppliers.

7. Read everything you can get your hands on regarding e-commerce and the changing world of technology.

* 21C.7   E-COMMERCE UPDATE

With the Gartner Group estimating that by 2005 well over half of all invoices will be delivered electronically, the issue is rapidly moving to the top of most accounts payable agendas. However, electronic invoice presentment and payment (EIPP), is not about the payment, says Hamish Forrest, Harris Bank's director of e-commerce solutions, dispelling a common myth; it's about the process. Speaking at IOMA's Advanced Accounts Payable Institute, Forrest described the two basic EIPP models and evaluated the advantages and disadvantages of each.

(a)   Background

Nowhere is the effect of the electronic evolution on the business community more evident than in the growing preponderance of acronyms used to describe everything—a practice many business-people find annoying. Forrest reviewed some of the more common ones:

- *EBPP and B2C.* Standing for *electronic bill presentment and payment* in the *business-to-consumer* environment, these represented the first phase in the electronic evolution.

- *EBPP and B2B.* This took the electronic revolution to the next level, by moving the concept into the *business-to-business* marketplace.

- *EIPP and B2B*. This expanded the process to include not only bills, but invoices, as well.

Some may think bills and invoices are the same thing, but this is not so. Invoices are those requests for payment, with many lines, sometimes differing prices, and, generally, terms. Invoices are often for large sums of money. A bill, in contrast, usually only has one or a few items listed; the prices are rarely subject to dispute; and a bill rarely involves terms. To put it in nontechnical terms, a bill resembles those requests you get personally for such things as phone service, office supplies, and so on.

On average, 60 percent of requests for payment at a company will be bills and 40 percent invoices. The Gartner Group estimates that each invoice that is moved into the electronic environment potentially saves an organization $7.15. Each year in the United States, 50 billion checks representing $47 trillion are written; 42 percent of that is B2B, a hefty opportunity for electronic innovations.

Several innovators in the marketplace, recognizing that the technology is here and the business community receptive, have been developing e-invoicing models. While each of the products has distinct bells and whistles, they fall into two broad categories: *biller-centric* and *payor-centric*.

(b)   Biller-Centric Model

The more prevalent models are biller-centric, meaning that the billing company drives them. It is a consolidator model that can include several options for the delivery of invoices. This might include EDI, paper, fax, and the Web. The goal of the billing company is to eliminate all paper invoices; and to do so, the biller may even offer the payor an incentive to convert.

In the biller-centric model, the purchaser visits the supplier's Web site to "pick up" its invoices. There is one major advantage related to biller-centric models: the online adjudication feature. Since all the relevant data is available on the supplier's site, purchasers can "drill down" for additional information needed to resolve disputes and discrepancies.

Payments can be made using the Automated Clearing House (ACH); the preferred methodology is by check, wire, or credit card.

(c) Payor-Centric Model

Payor-centric models are the reverse of the biller-centric models. Purchasers that desire to receive all invoices electronically, either via EDI or over the Internet, drive the transaction. They set up lockbox equivalents to receive invoices, either through imaging or data capture. As implied previously, there is no adjudication functionality. This model allows for decentralized approval process with a centralized mechanism. Forrest points out that this model can get some "quick hits" with B2B bills.

(d) Barriers to Implementation

If the benefits of these models are so pervasive, why haven't more companies adopted these solutions? The number-one reason, says Forrest, is the lack of integration between corporate accounting and the electronic payment systems. He also points out some additional obstacles, which include:

- Payment issues
- Technical drawbacks
- Education
- Existing business practices
- Lack of motivation and momentum

Since virtually everyone who works in accounts payable is not hampered by the last obstacle, EIPP offers a wonderful opportunity for them to take the lead and become the vanguard for the revolution that is taking place.

(e) Additional Benefits

Once the accounts payable professional has decided to try and advance the course of EIPP within his or her company, he or she can point out some of the following benefits:

- Reduced costs (remember the Gartner estimate of $7.15 per invoice)
- Ability to streamline accounts payable processes
- Opportunity to improve control and risk management, something that is high on corporate executives' agendas today
- Chance to improve strategic vendor relationships
- Ability to improve accuracy and timeliness of information

The cost reduction can be broken into two groups: business benefits and operational benefits. Forrest notes that the business benefits arise from the increased efficiencies when handling invoices, preparing checks, reviewing suspect items, imputing payment information to the accounts payable system, and the general ledger.

The operational benefits arise from a reduction in the handling of paper invoices and checks, reviewing suspect items, and the manual entry of payment information. Additionally, since electronic invoices don't get lost the way manual ones do, there should be a reduction in the number of rush checks required.

Forrest also noted that bank fees would be reduced, although he commented that this feature did not make bankers like him particularly happy. Archiving and mailing costs are also reduced with the advent of EIPP.

(f) What's in It for A/P?

By using EIPP, accounts payable departments can streamline many different parts of the invoice/bill-paying process. For starters, electronic distribution of information improves communication with vendors, and leverages other Web applications. Data entry errors are reduced, and the payment cycle can begin earlier. Thus, companies that have difficulties earning early payment discounts can easily overcome their former problems simply by taking advantage of the electronic distribution feature. Now, should someone in purchasing sit on an invoice for 30 days, there is a dated audit trail that clearly identifies who the culprit is.

In more than a few organizations, the accounts payable process bogs down as invoices are routed from one department or individual to the next. EIPP eliminates that problem as it automates the processing cycle. Companies can customize and automate business rules. They have the ability to automatically route and escalate if someone is out of the office or tardy in reviewing and approving where required. Everyone can see who did what, and when, something Forrest calls "visibility in the approval chain." The net result is a reduced incidence of lost and or delayed invoices and payments.

Electronic processing allows companies to accurately schedule payments to take advantage of early payment discounts and to pay in a timely manner. This means that in those instances where discounts are not available, the invoice is not paid early but rather scheduled for payment at an appropriate time. The last thing a company would want is to be so efficient that it pays its invoices weeks before the due date. This process allows companies to improve forecasting, make better use of trade credit, and reduce the number of late payments. This last factor eliminates the chance of being put on credit hold.

These improvements benefit companies greatly. It allows them to better manage their cash, reduce working capital requirements, and improve their credit ratings.

(g)   Additional A/P Benefits

From an accounts payable operational point of view, EIPP also decreases, if not eliminates, rush checks. It also reduces the number of manual entries required. In turn, this reduces the number of duplicate pays, bank stop payments, and the need to order new check stock and monitor the old. Check fraud also becomes less likely.

Finally, EIPP enables companies to improve their relationships with their vendors. While this may not be at the top of accounts payable professionals' priorities, it is usually very important to their companies.

Forrest closed his talk with a quote from Michael Hammer's *Reengineering the Corporation* (HarperCollins, 1993): "Obsessing over processes and getting them right is the only way a company can survive, especially now that the new economy has left early childhood and grown into a gangly unpredictable adolescent."

Are you ready?

Part Six

New Accounts
Payable Topics

22

Purchasing Cards

p. 268. Insert after carryover paragraph, before heading:

22.11A   TWO SUCCESS STORIES (NEW)

The recent *IOMA Benchmarking Survey* showed that 24% of the companies currently use p-cards, and another 32% plan to begin a program within the next year. Since this topic is so much on everyone's minds, here are two p-card success stories from the recent IOMA/IMI Managing Accounts Payable conference.

(a)   Purchasing Cards at Advanced Drainage Systems

Corporate accounts payable manager Mary Hurst knew there were too many invoices being processed by the company's accounts payable department. She ran a report and was able to determine that one third of the invoices processed were for under $150. The company went full force ahead with a purchasing card program. At the conference, she shared with the audience the following guidelines for establishing a successful p-card program:

- Decide who gets a card.
- Do not give cards to the clueless.
- Do give cards to those doing the purchasing.

- Set systems controls.
- Use softwares such as Smartdata for Windows or Procard for Windows.
- Use for purchasing, not travel and entertainment (T&E).
- Take a KISS (Keep It Simple, Silly) approach.
- Set realistic limits.
- Get top management support.
- Send a letter to vendors asking if they accept p-cards.
- Create a cardholder agreement.
- Have each cardholder keep a log.
- Load information from cardholder logs into Lotus Notes™.
- Use merchant category codes for mapping benefits.

In addition to reducing the number of invoices handled in the accounts payable department, Advanced Drainage Systems was also able to cut down on petty cash. Hurst reports that the average invoice was handled between seven and ten times, whereas a p-card payment is handled just twice.

(b) Purchasing Cards at Moody Bible Institute

Accounts payable-payroll administrator Roger Sipes knew there were too many invoices flowing through the accounts payable department. In this case, the Institute had begun using p-cards for invoices under $250 and planned eventually to move that dollar amount to $750. The institute established a task force from purchasing and accounts payable. Since it had several different types of businesses, representatives from each branch (broadcast, publishing, and retail) were represented. Sipes says that initially it was thought that using p-cards would eliminate the accounts payable department. Needless to say, that did not happen. Because the purchasing manager had experience with p-cards, he was chosen to lead the implementation effort. The company began its implementation in the spring of 1997 and hoped to have the project finished by year-end.

Y2K put an end to that plan, making it difficult to get management information systems (MIS) support. The company focused its efforts on identifying vendors capable of taking the card and developing a preferred supplier base. Sipes says he used the Internet to obtain information. When he had a problem, he simply went to one or more sites, such as IOMA's accounts payable discussion group and posted a question.

Like many other companies, the Institute found the biggest obstacle to be adequate accounting. The company looked at third-party software to handle the matter for them. They also went and visited another company already using the card and had the opportunity to play "devil's advocate." Thus, they were able to ensure that the accounts payable department's concerns were adequately addressed.

Sipes says that if he had to do it over again, he would become more involved in the rudimentary stage and would develop training material up front.

(c)   Lessons Learned

The starting point for any program is in the data. By running a simple report, one will be able to determine what dollar amount should be used to start a program. In the two cases studied here, $150 worked for the first company, while the second started with invoices under $250 and planned to move to a much higher number quickly.

Virtually everyone *Managing Accounts Payable* has encountered who has established such a program insists that there can never be too much planning or training. If you are involved in establishing a program at your company, try not to skimp on either of these phases.

Hurst (as well as many other professionals) recommends keeping purchasing cards separate from T&E activity. Some companies find they can get a rebate from the card issuer if they have sufficient volume and thus are combining activity. If you find your p-card activity high enough to qualify for such rebates, you might join the group that breaks this rule. If you have adequate controls and good accounting procedures in place, this should not cause you any problems.

Sipes reports running into trouble as Y2K dominates MIS resources. Expect that for the next year or two. Those professionals who are successful in establishing a program will be those who will learn how to do it without too much help from their MIS department.

22.11B   P-CARDS IN CANADA (NEW)

Many Canadian readers have called looking for information about p-cards in Canada. One of them took the same route as Roger Sipes in trying to find useful information. The following query was posted on the IOMA accounts payable discussion group: "I am currently looking for a p-card vendor for our two Canadian legal entities. Most U.S. companies cannot provide service in Canadian dollars. Can anyone help?"

Here's the advice that was offered:

- Having worked with Citibank on a couple of its recent wins (Ford and GM), they appear to have a strong offering in the Canadian market. You might want to try calling Colleen Dignam at 416-217-4094.
- We are in the early stages of developing a p-card program. From our initial research it looks like the bank of Montreal has the most advanced offering. Amex is also on the list. Most other Canadian Banks have limited programs.
- Royal Bank of Canada, which is in the process of buying Bank of Montreal, is the largest bank in Canada. They use Visa purchase cards. I attended one of their user conferences a couple of years ago and was impressed with the level of information imparted. I suggest you contact Kevin Jephcott at 416-974-8205.

p. 269. Insert at end of page:

22.13   A ROADMAP FOR SETTING UP
A P-CARD PROGRAM (NEW)

Setting up, monitoring, and evaluating a p-card program can be a bewildering experience for accounts payable professionals who have never ventured down this road. Speaking at the *Managing Accounts Payable* conference in Pasadena, Allergan Inc.'s Anita Breitzman provided a roadmap for the uninitiated. She walked the audience through the steps necessary to set up, evaluate, and manage a p-card program.

(a)   Establishing a Program

Senior management support is crucial to getting the rest of the company behind the program. Without it, the p-card program opponents will hinder implementation every step of the way. Interestingly enough, other accounts payable professionals report that the individuals who most opposed the p-card programs in their companies ultimately became their biggest supporters after participating in the programs for just a short time.

Once the goals have been set and quantified and management support is in place, a provider will have to be chosen. Ask hard questions of potential p-card providers. Network to find other accounts payable professionals who have card programs. Ask for recommendations and also find out the horror stories. Breitzman also recommends asking what your company will have to do to get started. Often, she says, the providers say they will help you, but when push comes to shove, the company must do more work than it initially anticipated. Find out exactly what will be expected of the company and then of the accounts payable staff—the amount of work could be substantial.

Like any other accounts payable process, a p-card program requires written, approved policies and procedures. Without them, the accounts payable manager responsible for the program will have huge headaches. When the program is new and unhampered by established bad habits on the part of card users, accounts payable professionals are in a position to get the program off on the right foot.

Always start with a pilot program. No matter how much planning goes into the project and how good the accounts payable staff is, there will be some rough spots in the beginning. This is not a time to be fair, says Breitzman. Pilot participants should be selected from those who support the program, not its detractors. There will be time to convert the skeptics later. You do not need them around should the pilot hit some bumps in the road. Once the pilot program has run for a while and the inevitable problems have been smoothed out, it is time to roll out the program to the rest of the company.

(b)   Evaluating the Program

Set measurable objectives in the implementation stage. After a reasonable amount of time, begin to quantify the results. Audit the information and get feedback from the p-card users. Ask the following questions:

- What has been learned
- What has been accomplished
- What additional issues should be addressed

Follow-up on the additional issues is recommended. Begin a regular benchmarking program and revise it as needed. Finally, Breitzman says that ongoing communication with the cardholders is crucial. This is the only way problems can be identified and corrected before they derail the p-card program.

(c)   Managing the Program

One of the great features of p-cards is that they allow the company to set controls for each employee as needed. To get started, establish card controls for each employee or group of employees as company policy dictates.

When interviewing potential card providers, discuss sales-and-use tax and 1099 reporting. The card provider (and they vary widely) must be integrated with accounts payable operations.

Work with the appropriate parties in accounting and information technology (IT) to establish whatever general ledger interface is desired. Different companies do it in different ways depending on the corporate preference and the capabilities of the accounting software used.

Establish a periodic reporting mechanism to keep management apprised of the success of the program and to provide others in the company with needed information.

Similarly, Breitzman recommends setting up an audit program to see if p-cards are being used as they should be and in all instances when they are supposed to be. Some accounts payable professionals have reported setting up a p-card program and then finding that those who objected to the program simply did not use the cards issued to them. Actions such as this can doom an otherwise good program to failure. Senior management support is key to enforcing usage in situations such as this. Some companies force p-card use by refusing to pay for items not charged to p-cards when applicable. This policy, of course, is extreme, and your company may not be willing to go this far.

Accounts payable professionals who rest on past successes are courting failure. Breitzman urges accounts payable professionals to continually look for expansion ideas. Where can accounts payable professionals find opportunities to expand their programs? In the first place, look to existing card users; they can often see additional uses for the cards. Breitzman also suggests going to user group meetings. By meeting with others using the same card program, accounts payable professionals will not only find unique solutions to their p-card problems, but will also discover innovative ways others are using the cards.

(d) P-Card Checklist

The following checklist can be used as a guide for a new p-card program, though some facets will always be company-specific.

(i) Establish a Program

1. Define goals and benefits.
2. Set measurable objectives.
3. Get senior management support.
4. Select p-card provider.
5. Establish policies and procedures.
6. Begin pilot program.
7. Roll out the program.

(ii) Evaluate the Program

1. Measure how objectives are being met.
2. Audit the results and user feedback.
3. Benchmark results and revise as needed.
4. Communicate with cardholders.

(iii) Manage the Program

1. Set card controls.
2. Administer sales and use tax.
3. Oversee 1099 reporting.
4. Take care of general ledger interface.
5. Set up reporting mechanisms.
6. Establish audit routine.
7. Look for expansion ideas.

* 22.14 THE ONE-CARD SOLUTION (NEW)

Rather than separate their p-cards from T&E cards, a growing number of companies are deciding to go the one-card route. Speaking at the IOMA/IMI Managing Accounts Payable conference, Diane McGuire, president of National Association of Purchasing Card Professionals, explained the advantages and disadvantages of this approach. The advantages include the convenience factor for the cardholders, the reduced system cost, and the ability to streamline negotiations with the card issues. On the other side of the coin, disadvantages include the liability issues; the belief that card issuers can provide better functionality if separate, tax compliance considerations; and the infrequent cardholder crossover. Those with large enough programs also see an advantage in combining the programs when the combination will allow the company to either qualify for a rebate or for a larger rebate when the programs are combined.

24

Benchmarking

24.3 SOME IOMA STATISTICS

p. 283. *Delete existing Exhibit 24.1 and replace with:*

Exhibit 24.1 **Vendor Payment Processing Costs**

Average Cost to Process a Payment	
Cost	**%**
$0–$5	44.8
$6–$10	21.0
$11–$15	11.5
$16–$20	4.7
$21–$25	4.5
$26–$50	9.3
Over $51	4.2
Average Cost to Process by Size of Company	
Up to 99	$14.81
100–249	$12.51
250–499	$13.20
500–999	$14.01
1,000–4,999	$14.29
Over 5,000	$10.62

Exhibit 24.1 (Continued)

Average Cost to Process by Industry	
Manufacturing	$15.18
Finance	$13.31
Utilities, transportation	$15.24
Private practice	$14.70
Nonprofit	$15.48
Wholesale/retail/distribution	$12.66
Health care	$10.96
Education	$ 7.25
Media	$16.18
Construction	$14.42
Entertainment/hospitality	$ 4.11
Other	$15.11

Source: IOMA.

24.4   BENCHMARKING APPLICATIONS

p. 285. Delete existing Exhibit 24.2 and replace with:

Exhibit 24.2   **Average Time to Process Invoices**

	Number of Days
Average	6.5
Median	4.0
Days	**%**
0–2.9	23.4
3–5.9	45.8
6–10.9	18.1
11–20.9	7.4
Over 21	5.2
Average Time by Number of Employees	*Days*
Up to 99	6.9
100–249	6.8
250–499	7.1
500–999	6.6
1,000–4,999	6.5
Over 5,000	5.3
Average Time by Industry	*Days*
Manufacturing	5.6
Finance	5.6
Utilities, transportation	7.0
Private practice	7.2
Nonprofit	9.5
Wholesale/retail/distribution	6.4
Health care	6.5
Education	5.6
Media	7.0
Construction	7.5
Entertainment/hospitality	6.6
Other	6.9

Source: IOMA.

p. 288. Insert at end of chapter:

24.5   DAYS TO PAY (NEW)

One of the ways accounts payable departments are measured is through the use of a calculation called days payable outstanding (DPO). Although there is a traditional financial analysis calculation for this concept, accounts payable professionals are using their own variations of this old tool to measure their own performance and that of their staff.

(a)   Textbook Calculations

Financial analysts look at the DPO calculation to determine how a company is paying its trade creditors. The DPO is calculated by taking the trade accounts payable figure and dividing it by credit purchases. That result is then divided by 360. If the credit purchase figure is not available, then total annual purchases are used. To make an accurate assessment of this figure, it should be compared to industry averages.

Some chief financial officers feel that an increasing DPO figure gives the impression that the company is experiencing financial difficulties. Thus, they direct their staffs to keep it under a certain level. Keep this in mind if you work for a publicly traded company and want to recommend payment stretching.

(b)   Days-to-Pay Variation

Accounts payable professionals interested in benchmarking department performances are more apt to track a figure that has been loosely dubbed "days to pay." The simplest way to do this is to calculate the number of days between the invoice date and the check date. The problem with this method is that the accounts payable department gets tagged for any mail delays. Also, a few companies have been known to predate invoices so their customers will pay earlier than they need to. The days to pay calculation can be averaged by both numbers of invoices and dollar amount.

(c) One Variation

Here is how one company uses this formula: We calculate the difference between the invoice date and paid date to get total days outstanding for each invoice during the period. We then total the days for all invoices and divide by the number of invoices. We try to stay at 30 days outstanding. We exclude some payments from the calculation like tax payments, employee reimbursements, and so on.

Although this methodology has its merits, the accounts payable department may end up with a number that indicates performance which is worse than it actually is. Accounts payable professionals should be aware that many companies perform separate calculations for trade vendors and employee travel and entertainment reimbursements.

(d) Outside Internal Problems

As those reading this know only too well, accounts payable's performance time can be greatly inhibited by the actions, or lack thereof, of others. The best accounts payable performance can be thwarted by the purchasing manager who takes 45 days to return invoices with his approval for payment. Recognizing this problem, one accounts payable manager has crafted a solution around it.

"The majority of our invoices require approval, he writes on the IOMA discussion group. Therefore, to get an accurate picture of the performance of the accounts payable area, we break out 'invoice date to be received by accounts payable' and 'received to paid date.' This allows us to track the amount of time the invoice takes for approval, as well as processing time," he concludes. The beauty of this approach is that it not only removes the onus of others' behavior from the accounts payable benchmarking number, but it arms the accounts payable manager with information needed to go after laggard approvers.

(e) Using These Numbers

Days to pay numbers are quite useful in proving the efficiency of the accounts payable department. The IOMA benchmarking survey showed that, on average, it takes accounts payable five days to pay an invoice. That is five days once the invoice arrives in the accounts department. As indicated above, there are a number of issues that can make these numbers murky if tracking is done from the invoice date.

"We use the number of days between the date received into accounts payable and the date entered into the system for payment," explains another accounts payable professional in the IOMA discussion group. "The clock does not start ticking unless that invoice is prepared according to our policies and procedures. We then have service levels of four days to process expense reports and five days to process regular payable invoices from the date received," she concludes. How important are these numbers? At this company these figures are used in calculating staff bonuses.

In some companies, accounts payable is the scapegoat for everyone else's errors. It is easy to blame accounts payable for delays in payments when the truth is that the invoice sat on someone's desk or was submitted with incorrect figures. Armed with days to pay and/or DPO numbers, the accounts payable manager can refute such allegations and defend the department. Once people see that accounts payable will not take the blame for others' mistakes, the attitude toward the accounts payable department will change. While this improvement in reputation will not take place overnight, it will occur if the accounts payable manager and staff keep up the attack.

Several accounts payable managers report that their companies use these figures to control cash flow. They do this by comparing the DPO figure with the net terms to determine how good a job the company is doing at earning discounts. However the accounts payable professional decides to use the data benchmarking numbers will provide the ammunition needed to support the accounts payable manager's recommendations.

* 24.5A   CASE STUDY: THE ABCs OF METRICS: HOW TO START OR IMPROVE A GOOD BENCHMARKING PROGRAM (NEW)

Most accounts payable professionals know they should be benchmarking the performance of their departments. Many do a fine job; however, a few have confided that they don't know where to start. To help those readers, along with those who are looking to tweak their existing benchmarking processes, we invited two metrics experts from the Gap to share their benchmarking experiences at a recent IOMA/IMI Managing Accounts Payable conference. Not only did Debbie Vander Bogart, the Gap's director, and Bennae Stanfield, manager, explain the basics, they also pointed out some of the pitfalls to avoid when establishing a benchmarking program.

(a)   Background

The two speakers immediately put the audience at ease by revealing that when they first started attending accounts payable conferences they didn't know what metrics were. They've come a long way. They pointed out that benchmarking, like so many other things in accounts payable, is an evolutionary process that takes time. They also said that they still feel like they are learning when it comes to metrics.

The two pointed out that it's crucial that the benefits be communicated with the staff—the "what's in it for them" factor. If you are wondering what's in it for the staff, the answer is simple: By having the counts, you can justify headcount and new projects (and the staff to do them). The speakers suggested that the work of the accounts payable staff is not the only thing that should be measured. If you send out invoices for approval, you should also measure how long different people or departments hold on to invoices.

(b)   The Process

Vander Bogart and Stanfield pointed out that benchmarking has many advantages. In addition to being able to justify headcounts, projects, and so on, the procedure helps improve existing processes and eliminate inefficiencies in the accounts payable department. It also flushes out other issues that might not have surfaced without close inspection. For example, if someone on the staff is making extra copies or looking up G/L codes that should be handled by purchasing, the issue will surface during the flow-chart stage. More than one accounts payable manager experienced a real eye-opener during the documentation phase.

Here are the 10 steps the speakers use in their benchmarking process. Readers interested in benchmarking can examine it closely either to develop a plan that will work in their own companies or to fine-tune their own processes.

1. *Set objectives.* The speakers recommended that the process be used to establish both quality and service indicators and that the initial goals be relatively simple to measure. Once you are comfortable with the process, you can go after the more complicated metrics.

2. *Market your program before you begin.* "Build up for a big launch" is the recommendation of the experts from the Gap. Make sure everyone knows what you are going to do and what your objectives are. For example, set a quality goal that says you will process invoices within five days of receiving them in the accounts payable department.

3. *Identify your current processes.* They might not be what you think they are. The speakers suggest that you flowchart the full process for your department. Don't do it from memory; rather, follow the workflow through the department. They also strongly recommend that you break out each individual task in the process.

4. *Include the entire staff in observations.* Time and motion studies will not be believed if only a few people are included. The speakers noted that they learned the hard way that standing with a stopwatch timing the staff is not going to be a positive experience for anyone involved. They suggest picking a 15-minute time frame and simply counting how many invoices are processed. Be creative when establishing the metrics, and try and have some fun.

5. *Create, calculate, and update worksheets* once the metrics have been agreed upon.

6. *Share the results of the benchmarking endeavor with the entire staff.* It is imperative that the results of the project be communicated with those being measured. Be creative and avoid finger-pointing.

7. *Review the workflow charts to identify those areas that can be eliminated or reworked to be more efficient.* Each person will have his or her own way of performing the same task. By taking the best from each, it may be possible to develop an incredibly efficient procedure. Don't forget to ask the staff for input at this point. The people doing the work usually have very good ideas about how the work they do every day can be improved.

8. *Establish customer service agreements between the accounts payable department and your internal business partners.* This can be based on the criteria you have established through your metrics. The speakers suggested that these agreements should be tailored to the individual requirements of the businesses. Accounts payable departments that handle different divisions may do very different work for each division.

9. *Set a specific calendar for the ongoing evaluation of the metrics.* Continue observing, measuring, and most importantly, communicating the results with the staff. Make sure the staff understands that you are simply trying to tweak the system to make it as efficient as possible, not to take punitive action against anyone.

10. *Periodically review your actual processes against your flowcharts.* Why? Because without realizing it, the staff will gradually change the process, incorporate some shortcuts, and possibly come up with even better ways of doing things. Alternatively, some bad habits may sneak in and you want to be in a position to identify those practices and stop them as quickly as possible.

(c) A Few Pointers

Both Stanfield and Vander Bogart noted that benchmarking can become an overwhelming project, if you let it. Don't let the project take over, or you *will* get frustrated. Understand that it will take time, especially if you want to do it right. But don't let that deter you—the sooner you get started, the sooner you will get finished.

Sometimes, benchmarking puts off the staff. They feel they are being watched and treated like factory workers. The key to preventing such misconceptions is communication and marketing. It can mean the difference between the success and failure of your benchmarking program.

Realize that it will take time if it is to be successful. And whenever you have successes—*and you will*—make sure you celebrate them with your staff—no matter how big or small. The speakers shared some of the ways they celebrate at the Gap's accounts payable department. Ice cream and balloons were two simple ways the staff was thanked for outstanding efforts. Doughnuts were also mentioned.

In an effort to have some fun—yes, some accounts payable departments do have fun—the Gap took its accounts payable department outside for a picnic and some brainstorming. The two speakers brought with them squishy stress balls in the shape of a heart. The balls, which have "I love Accounts Payable" printed on them, are given to internal customers, especially those who might have issues with accounts payable.

Benchmarking is not easy. However, it can provide accounts payable managers with the ammunition to get what they need for both the department and the staff. This alone makes it worth the time and effort. Have you started yet?

24.6 HOW ONE ACCOUNTS PAYABLE PROFESSIONAL USES METRICS TO IMPROVE PRODUCTIVITY AND HER DEPARTMENT'S IMAGE (NEW)

When most accounts payable professionals contemplate benchmarking, they think only of comparing their numbers to the results at other similar companies. However, this is just one type of benchmarking. Using metrics to gauge your department's productivity and progress is a more useful measurement approach used at leading companies today. At RECAP's recent "Enhancing Accounts Payable" conference, Sandy Campos described how she uses metrics to improve the accounts payable department at Charles Schwab.

(a)   Why Measure?

For starters, Campos says using metrics helps evaluate the current situation in the department while allowing the manager to establish quantifiable goals for each staff member as well as the department as a whole. With quantifiable results, the manager is then able to communicate successes to management. It is much easier to prove that the department has improved when you have hard numbers to back up your assertions.

These figures also give the ammunition needed to focus and direct staff. The data provides a starting point to motivate performance and uncover inefficiencies both within and outside the department. Campos gave an example of posting the level of a backlog. From the backlog figures, it was possible to locate bottlenecks in the process. Noteworthy is the fact that in quite a few organizations that holdup is in the approval process. Finally, Campos says that she uses benchmarking to foster a team environment.

(b)   How to Measure

Once accounts payable managers become convinced of the need to benchmark, they want to know how a successful director of disbursement services like Campos manages the process at Schwab. She provides the following guidelines:

- Create simple measurements.
- Provide data in real time.
- Give others input into measurements.
- Query the accounts payable database.
- Use benchmark data to confirm measurements and establish goals.

- Use individual and team measurements.
- Use internal and external measurements.

Benchmarking internal operations is not a one-shot affair. "Measuring often will ensure you are up-to-date with your department's current situation," says Campos. A sharp decline in processor productivity will show up quickly if numbers are tabulated daily or weekly. She says that the frequency of your benchmarking activity will depend on what you are measuring; it can be as often as daily or as infrequently as quarterly.

Another factor in the frequency equation is the ease of compiling data. If it is possible to pull the information from the existing accounting information, you can prepare your reports more often than the accounts payable manager who must create the reports from scratch.

(c)   What Should Be Measured?

Ask 20 managers what metric is most important at their companies, and you will get 20 different answers. Campos recommends determining what the key drivers are to your business and measuring them. Discounts lost might be very important to a company that operates on thin margins while it might be insignificant to those who rarely offer discounts.

She suggests classifying the types of measurements in quality, productivity, or volume metrics. The number of errors is an example of a quality metric while the level of the backlog is an illustration of a productivity measurement. Campos suggests that accounts payable managers should measure what is easy to act on and is easy to understand. She gives some examples of what accounts payable managers might use:

- Dun & Bradstreet Paydex Rating
- Processor productivity
- Accounts payable expenses per voucher
- End-of-month backlog

- Processor error rates
- Electronic billing as a percentage of total processing

Those who have entered the imaging age might also track their backlogs broken into the following three categories:

1. Waiting to be scanned
2. Waiting to be indexed
3. Waiting to be processed

(d) Using Metrics to Prod Other Departments

One of the problems many accounts payable professionals have is getting managers in other areas to return invoices approved for payment. Campos has an interesting solution to this issue and she uses metrics as the first step.

She begins by tracking invoice approval time. Once a week, she sends an e-mail to senior executives with this information. However, she does not include all the data in the body of the e-mail. She sends the report as an attachment and uses the body of the e-mail for "highlights." She uses this approach to embarrass those who are slow to return approved invoices for payment.

Occasionally, she calls the boss of a tardy manager to get the ball rolling. Interestingly enough, she says that she rarely has to make these calls anymore. Getting the approved invoices back for payment quickly reduces the number of rush checks. Why? These laggards make up a good portion of those demanding an immediate check to pay vendors who are threatening not to ship.

(e) Other Benefits

Many accounts payable managers face a challenge in how the rest of the company views their department. Often unfairly, the department has a shoddy reputation. By using metrics to communicate successes to senior management, you can take a big step toward projecting a positive professional image for yourself and your department.

Part Seven

Other Accounts
Payable Topics

25

1099s

25.6 B-NOTICES

p. 295. Add after fourth full paragraph:

(b) B-Notice

Most accounts payable professionals who are responsible for sending out 1099s have also had the dubious pleasure of sending B-notices. While most reading this know how to issue 1099s, many are not as well versed in what they must do and when they do not have to send a B-notice. Attendees at RECAP's "Enhancing Accounts Payable" conference were fortunate enough to hear the American Payroll Association's (APA) James J. Medlock (a.k.a. "Mr. 1099") address this issue.

(c) What Is a B-Notice?

Payments made to independent contractors must be reported to the federal government in the beginning of the year for the prior year. These amounts are also reported to the independent contractor on a 1099. The contractor is then required to include those amounts in his or her income tax calculations. The problem arises when the tax identification number (TIN) provided does not match the name reported.

Should this occur, the lucky accounts payable manager will receive a CP2100A notice from the Internal Revenue Service (IRS). You should be aware that the IRS will report that the TIN is missing. The IRS considers a TIN to be missing when the one provided does not match the name on its records and when the number provided is obviously incorrect. So, even though you provided a TIN, you will still be notified that one was missing. You are then required to send a B-notice to the independent contractor. There are three kinds of B-notices: the first, second, and third (or subsequent).

(d)   First Notice

After reviewing your records to ensure that you did not make the mistake, you should also review your records to see if this is the first time that you are being notified about this particular individual. Your subsequent actions will depend on the answer to this inquiry. Assuming that this is the first occurrence, send a letter to the independent contractor along with a W-9 form.

Medlock also recommends sending along a self-addressed, stamped reply envelope. The APA suggests that the envelope in which the letter and W-9 form are sent be marked prominently to the effect that important tax information is contained in the package.

(e)   Second Notice

The second time the IRS notifies you, different steps must be taken. However, the IRS will not tell you that this is a second notice. You will need to check your records to determine if the IRS has notified you about this particular taxpayer within the last three years. After checking your records and determining that you have been notified about this particular taxpayer and you did send the first B-notice, prepare a second B-notice. It is not necessary to send along another W-9.

Medlock suggests sending along an optional reply envelope. He also recommends marking the outside of the envelope to indicate what is enclosed. Language such as "Important Tax Return

Document Enclosed" should be marked clearly on the outside of the envelope.

Keep very detailed and accurate records of these transactions. Should the envelope be returned, keep it in your files. Try and find the correct address for the taxpayer. If you do, send the notice again.

The APA strongly discourages taking this information verbally. By getting the information in writing, the taxpayer certifies that the TIN is correct. If the taxpayer does not respond, the company then is required to begin withholding 31% of payments made to that individual as backup withholding taxes. The notice to the company can come in the form of an SSA Form 7028 or an IRS letter 147C. Either must be received within 30 days in order to avoid the withholding.

(f)   Third and Subsequent Notices

Once again, it will be necessary to check prior-year records to determine what notice is being received. If it is the third or subsequent notice, then no action is required if the name and TIN reported are the same as in prior years. However, if the combination is not the same, you must treat the notice as a first notice and begin the process again.

Many thought getting the W-9 was the battle and, in many cases, it is. However, having received the W-9 may not be the end of the fight. As can be seen from Medlock's talk, if the information reported does not match what the IRS has on its records, the accounts payable manager's job is not complete.

This piece is a short synopsis of the requirements for accounts payable managers responsible for issuing 1099s. Those looking for more information about B-notices can visit the American Payroll's Web site, *www.americanpayroll.org,* or purchase its excellent book, *Accounts Payable Preparing for Year End and 2000.*

p. 297. Insert at end of chapter:

25.11 SELECTING NEW 1099 SOFTWARE (NEW)

Are you looking to get rid of that old clunky software that produces your 1099s? If you are not satisfied with your 1099 policy, procedures, or software, the time to deal with those issues is long before year end rolls around.

(a) Identifying the Problem

Sit back and mentally review how the year-end 1099 process went. If everything ran smoothly, thank the powers that be for including you in that small group of accounts payable professionals who didn't see a few more hairs turn gray over this issue. Assuming you were not one of the lucky few, list the problems you had. Review the list and determine whether the problems can be fixed by one of the following:

- Procedural change within the accounts payable department
- Additional training
- Policy change
- Procedural change that involves other departments
- New software

(b) Fixing the Problem

If the problems can be fixed by one of the first two solutions listed in subsection (a), you should be able to solve them on your own. However, if those were the best solutions, most A/P professionals would have already employed them. We suspect that most of the solutions lie in one of the last three categories on the list. If this is the case, decide who you need to contact and begin the process now.

If you need new 1099 software, visit the Web sites listed here (or call some of the phone numbers listed) to obtain more information about programs available to help issue 1099s. The software listed here is not the only software available. It is simply a short list to get you started.

- *www.1099pro.com/* 888-PRO-1099
- *www.bockmon.com/* 830-281-6759
- *easiamerica.com/* 770-232-1865
- *www.alpinedata.com/tpw2_a.htm/* 800-525-1040
- *www.1099online.com/*

If management will not allocate the money needed to purchase this software, you might try hitting them with the overtime costs associated with issuing 1099s last year. That one number may help them see the light.

* 25.12   IT'S 1099 TIME: NEW CHANGES IMPLEMENTED IN 2002 (NEW)

Never the easiest task facing the accounts payable professional, 1099s continue to head the list of migraine-provoking year-end projects. The IRS, in its attempt to capture more information, identify possible tax cheats, and, at least in theory, make things easier for those issuing the detested forms, has instituted some changes for 2002. Speaking at several recent conferences, Balance Consulting's research director Marianne Couch and Michael Boyle delineated some of these changes and offered excellent advice on the general issuance of Form 1099s.

(a)   Background

There are two philosophies when it comes to 1099s. The one Balance Consulting recommends is the so-called how-to-be-safe approach; but they concede that there is a whole group of companies that take the what-can-we-get-away-with approach to 1099s. As most readers are painfully aware, companies should get taxpayer identification numbers (TIN) before paying an independent contractor. If the TIN is not provided, law requires back-up withholding of 30 percent. This can be a real hassle for companies, because not only does the money have to be withheld, it also has to be turned over to the IRS. So most accounts payable departments do whatever they can to get the TIN.

NOTE: The withholding requirement for 2002 and 2003 is 30 percent. The rate will fall to 29 percent for 2004 and 2005 and 28 percent for 2006 through 2009. The rate then jumps to 31 percent for tax years starting in 2010—unless the tax code is changed again (and what are the odds of that?).

Expect a renewed focus on TINs. They can be one of the following:

- SSN
- EIN
- ITIN (for foreign workers)
- ATIN (for adopted babies before an SSN is issued)

ITINs are relatively easy to recognize. They look like Social Security numbers but begin with a 9. Since September 11, 2001, there has been a greater interest in aliens, and this trickles into the 1099 world. Greater emphasis is being put on Form 1042-S, which companies will be required to file when payments are made to aliens. Expect more of an emphasis on this issue in the next few years.

(b) A Few Words about W-9s

As most readers are aware, W-9s are the form used by many companies to obtain TINs. When setting up a new vendor, you must use a form that was revised January 2002. This refers to the correct back-up withholding rate and directs nonresident aliens to use Form W-8. Whether you use the government W-9 form or create your own substitute W-9 form, it must contain a statement that says, "Use this form only if you are a U.S. person." All companies using their own W-9 forms (i.e., substitute W-9s) must make sure this statement is on their substitute W-9s.

(c) New IRS TIN Matching System

One of the many problems accounts payable professionals have with 1099s is the fact that numerous independent contractors provide TINs that do not match the name they have provided. The proverbial DBA (doing business as), the minor misspellings, and other assorted clerical issues all lead to additional work in accounts payable. If there were a way to verify this information upfront, life would be a little easier for the accounts payable professionals handling 1099s. Now there is.

As this goes to print, the IRS is unveiling a new system that allows registered payors to submit a list of names and TINS to the IRS for verification prior to the filing deadline. Couch indicates that payors will have two methods for submitting names and the matching TINs to see if they are accurate per the IRS.

1. Using an interactive session, up to 25 requests can be submitted per session. *Response time*:   seconds. *Availability*: Possibly November 2003.

2. Bulk submissions of up to 100,000 requests can be submitted per session. *Response time*: 24 hours. *Availability*: Possibly May 2003.

NOTE: Use of either of these systems requires registration. If you are interested in participating, Boyle suggests that you send Sharon Wilson of the IRS an e-mail, at *sharon.y.wilson@irs.gov*, indicating that you want to participate. Alternatively, you can call her at 304-264-5777.

Here's how it will work: The payor will provide the name and TIN of the payee, and the IRS will respond with one of the following codes:

0 = Name and TIN match
1 = TIN missing or not nine digits
2 = TIN not currently issued
3 = TIN/name combination does not match
4 = Invalid request
5 = Duplicate request

Watch out for those 5s. If the IRS suspects you are on a fishing expedition, warns Couch, it will cut off your access for 96 hours. The beauty of these systems is that if they are used on an ongoing basis, the accounts payable professional will be able to determine that the TIN does not match the name, and the correct information can be obtained *before* the vendor is paid—when you still have some leverage.

(d) Electronic Posting of Statements

Effective February 14, 2001, the U.S. Treasury gave companies the option of posting payee statements electronically, rather than mailing statements. Couch notes that this process is not yet available for contributions and distributions of pensions, traditional IRAs, Coverdell ESAs, Roth IRAs, and Archer MSAs.

The IRS requires consent and disclosure. The electronic version of the statement must contain all the required information and comply with applicable rules relating to the creation of substitute statements. The statements must be posted on a Web site that is accessible to recipients on or before January 31. The information must be maintained and accessible until at least October 15 or 90 days after any correction is posted, whichever is later.

Boyle noted that this allows companies that obey all the rules and regulations to post their 1099s on their Web sites, as long as they get the needed approvals upfront. He says that Balance and other companies will do this for companies interested in this process.

Accounts payable professionals who are aware of these changes are in the best position to make sure their companies comply with all the applicable regulations. Those who take advantage of the electronic matching offered by the IRS will make their year-end 1099 work a lot easier—now let's just hope the IRS can get the program up and running quickly.

25A

Sales and Use Tax (New)

Tax laws are rarely simple or easily understandable. Sales tax rules are among the most complicated and arcane of the lot. Not only do they vary from state to state but even among counties and sometimes even among towns within the same state. Failure to pay proper sales and/or use tax can result in fines. States have been stepping up their sales and use tax audits in an attempt to generate income without raising taxes on the residents who vote. It is a painless way for states to increase revenues without offending voters. Worse, states cooperate with each other, so a company that gets a visit from one state auditor is likely to be visited again—if it is found to be negligent. In some cases, auditors work for more than one state.

In four out of five companies it is the accounts payable department that handles this function, not the tax department. Accounts payable professionals must analyze all invoices to ensure that the proper tax has been paid. If it has not, they need to make sure the seller adjusts the invoice and pays it or that their company pays the necessary use tax.

Sales tax cannot be assessed in a jurisdiction if the seller does not have substantial physical presence. This does not mean that no sales tax must be paid. Never let it be said that Uncle Sam let a few bucks get away. It simply transfers the responsibility for collecting and paying that tax to the appropriate party. That is where use tax comes in. Each state has its own rules about that as well. Are you getting a headache yet?

25A.1 WHAT IS SALES AND USE TAX?

Sales tax is a tax on the retail sale of tangible personal property. It is important to note that it should be paid only on retail sales. It is also charged on certain services. Use tax is a little more complicated. It is charged by many (but not all) states on the "privilege of storing." In this case, storage means when the purchaser holds or controls property brought in from out of state that is not intended for resale. Generally speaking, if goods are to be used for demonstration or display, they are not subject to use tax. The rules for what is subject to use tax and what is not are very complicated and vary from state to state. It is imperative that the accounts payable professionals responsible for sales and use tax learn what his or her state rules are.

25A.2 EDUCATION

Start by knowing what theories apply to your states. Sections 25A.5 and 25A.6 contain descriptions of sales and use tax types. While at first glance these items may seem inconsequential, do not be fooled. In order to calculate a company's sales and use tax liability, these concepts must be analyzed for each state from which the company buys. Any company that buys or sells goods outside its own boundaries is required to know the sales and use tax laws of all the states involved.

There are a number of ways that accounts payable professionals with this responsibility can get themselves up the learning curve on sales and use tax. Padgett Thompson/AMA offers both a one- and two-day sales and use tax seminar at which participants are given advice relating to sales and use tax. Dates of local seminars can be obtained by calling 800-255-4141 or visiting *www.amanet.org/seminars/public.* Those interested in detailed information about each state can access that state's Web site.

As of May 1999 the following states have no sales and use tax:

- Alaska
- Delaware
- Montana
- New Hampshire
- Oregon

If you are located in those states, it does not automatically mean having no sales and use tax responsibilities. You may be required to pay or collect the tax to other locales depending on the nature of your business.

One excellent source of free information on the Internet is the Sales Tax Institute. *(www.salestaxinstitute.com/).* The company offers sales and use tax seminars for a reasonable fee also. This site contains periodic updates of information useful to those responsible for sales and use tax.

25A.3   POLICIES AND PROCEDURES

A few companies have no formal policies and procedures for the sales and use tax responsibility. An auditor who finds a company in noncompliance is likely to be more sympathetic to a company that has a policy in place than one who has ignored the issue. The existence of a policy indicates that the company intends to pay its sales and use taxes even if it does not always do it correctly. The lack of a formal policy implies the company has no plan to pay. Thus, the existence of a policy is a company's first defense against an aggressive tax collector.

Even those with a policy need to revise and update it periodically as the laws continually change. Finally, there is one last reason to have a policy in place and that is the communication that goes on between states and between the differing taxing authorities within one state. Many in the field believe this information is freely exchanged. Once a company is hit for back payments and penalties, the likelihood is that other taxing authorities will come knocking at their doors.

25A.4 SALES AND USE TAX AUDITS

Some accounts payable professionals dread sales and use tax audits because they do not know what to expect and are not sure that their companies are complying with sales and use laws 100% of the time. These conditions can be alleviated (or at least made bearable) through education and a thorough update of corporate sales and use tax policies and procedures.

(a) What to Expect in an Audit

At its seminar on this topic Padgett Thompson/AMA indicates that accounts payable professionals can expect the following four stages in any sales and use tax audit:

1. Examination of sales
2. Examination of purchases
3. Balancing of the general ledger sales and use tax accounts
4. Review of journal voucher transactions

The examination of the purchases can be further broken down into the following three stages:

1. Purchases delivered into the taxpayer's state from out of state on which the seller did not collect tax
2. Purchases in which the taxpayer gave the seller an exemption certification where the property was not used in the manner for which the exemption was given
3. Purchases in a nonseller privilege tax state where the seller failed to collect the tax at the time of the sale

The auditors will either do detail auditing or sample auditing. Should a notice for a sales and use tax audit be received at an inconvenient time, ask to reschedule to a time that works better. This tactic should not be used as an avoidance technique because the day of reckoning will come and inevitably at an even worse time.

(b)   Handling the Auditors

Effective handling of sales and use tax auditors is not really complicated: treat them courteously. Give them a decent place to work without giving them the best or the worst work location. The auditors should not be given free access to all the company records. There is a more common-sense way to handle the matter.

Assign one person to be the focal point for all auditor inquiries. Let that person do whatever is necessary to get the auditor the needed information. This could include:

- Searching the files for documents
- Asking other people within the company for information
- Researching issues

The goal of this approach is to ensure that the auditor is not antagonized nor given unnecessary information. Most importantly, do not offer information not asked for. The last thing that any accounts payable professional should do is open a door to an issue that the auditor has not seen fit to investigate. If the auditor misses something, it is not the company's responsibility to point it out.

Sales and use tax audits are one of those pesky annoying tasks that cannot be avoided. By being well informed and facing them head on, you will find that the anticipation of the audit is actually much worse than the audit itself. Are you ready?

25A.5   CHARACTERISTICS

Shifting—The economic burden of paying the tax is "shifted" to the buyer.

Absorption—The right of the seller to "absorb" the payment of the tax on behalf of the buyer, thereby making the tax a competitive tool of price negotiation.

Separation—The tax amount must appear as a "separate" line item on an invoice or receipt from other elements of a sales transaction.

25A.6   TYPES

Seller privilege—The seller has the privilege of selling and is liable for the tax measured by the taxable sales.

Consumer levy—The buyer has the privilege of buying and is liable for the tax with the seller serving as the trustee or agent of the state in collecting the tax.

Transaction—The transaction has the privilege with the buyer liable for the tax imposed upon the transaction. In the seller's failure to add tax to the buyer's invoice, the buyer and seller remain jointly liable.

Gross receipt—The seller has the privilege and is liable for the tax measured by the taxable sales.

25A.7   KEEPING UP TO DATE

By now, it is probably obvious that the person responsible for sales and use tax needs to follow the issues closely. Luckily, there is much information available. Here are some places to find it:

On the Internet. Those readers interested in weekly updates to individual state sales and use tax rulings can visit *http://www.-riatax.com/weekly/state.html* to find the latest information.

Online delivery of sales and use tax rate information is also available via Research Institute of America's (RIA) Checkpoint product. For more information call 800-431-9025, ext. 3.

In Books

All States Tax Guide—Find fast answers to state tax questions. This book simplifies doing business in several states. It contains more than 400 pages' worth of charts, checklists, and state-by-state comparisons. Valuable lists of official state contacts with addresses and phone numbers. Cost: approximately $30.

1999 Guide to Sales and Use Taxes—(Annual) Cost: approximately $60.

Georgia Sales and Use Tax Laws—Amazon.com, price: $16.00, paperback, 128 pages, 1998 edition, Lexis Law Publishing.

Florida, Louisiana, etc.—These other states have published their own books on the topic. Some of them are available on Amazon.com, but care should be taken with the information if the publication is not up-to-date.

In Newsletters. Both Bureau of National Affairs (BNA) and IOMA offer newsletters devoted exclusively to sales and use tax. To find more information about these publications visit the following Web sites:

- *www.ioma.com*
- *www.bna.com*

25A.8   USE TAX AND NEXUS

How are you supposed to know if your vendors have triggered nexus in your state, and, if they have not, why should it be your concern? Nexus is the states' way of determining if a company has a "physical presence" in the state. Knowing how nexus is triggered and what your vendors are doing about it will put you in the best position to make sure your company is paying all the sales and/or use tax it is obligated to pay. It is always the buyer's obligation to pay, regardless of whether its vendors collect and remit it as sales tax. If the seller does not collect it, the buyer is expected to remit it in the form of use tax. Therefore, it is imperative that accounts payable professionals fully understand all the implications of nexus.

(a)   Physical Presence

Just checking in the telephone book to see if a vendor has a listing is not enough to guarantee that a company has or does not have a *physical presence*. At the AMA seminar, the factors that might trigger sufficient nexus necessary to subject a nonresident seller to a state's sales and use tax laws were spelled out. They include:

- Ownership in the form of inventory or equipment
- Ownership of a billboard

- A company maintaining a building (office, warehouse, retail store, etc.)
- Lease or rental facilities
- Presence of an affiliate (parent, subsidiary, brother, or sister)
- Participation in a trade show

25A.9 SPECIALIZED SOFTWARE

Several companies offer software that can be used to track sales and use tax. They include:

- Vertex Inc., *www.vertexinc.com/*
- DPC, *www.salestax.com/*
- Taxware International, *www.taxware.com/*. This company has a user group meeting scheduled for the end of August 2000 in Boston.
- Weiss Group, *www.exemptiontracker.com/*

25A.10 ADDITIONAL LEARNING OPPORTUNITIES

As you can see, nexus can be difficult to determine. In fact, everything connected with sales and use tax is involved. Attendance at seminars such as the ones run by Padgett Thompson/AMA will help those who have responsibility for this important function. Here is contact information for several organizations that run sales and use tax seminars.

- Padgett Thompson/AMA, 800-262-9699, *www.amanet.org*
- Baker, Shore & Associates, Ltd., 716-439-6320, *http://www.bakershore.com/* (this company also offers courses in Canada)
- The Sales Tax Institute, 312-986-1086, *www.salestaxinstitute.com*

25A.11   KEEP YOUR COWORKERS FROM MAKING YOUR SALES AND USE TASKS HARDER

Administering the sales and use tax function for a company is no easy task for accounts payable professionals. For one thing, the regulations vary dramatically from state to state, making it impossible for multistate businesses to design any sort of standardized approach to determining sales and use tax liability. What might be a smart tax move in one jurisdiction, for example, may not work, or may even backfire, in another.

Perhaps more frustrating, costly, and difficult to contain, however, are the sales and use tax ramifications of decisions regularly made by employees in nontax departments. Although these can be significant, many decision makers are unaware of the existence of sales and use taxes, let alone their impact. *Result:* Accounts payable is left to clean up messes that might have been avoided.

(a)   Gather Information

What can accounts payable managers do to better administer the sales and use tax function? Become an information gatherer, says Diane Yetter, president of Yetter Consulting Services, Inc. Also the founder of the Sales Tax Institute (*www.salestaxinstitute*), Yetter suggests the following steps:

- *Collect as much information as possible from as many sources as possible.* This information can be used to determine nexus, evaluate taxability, prepare returns, defend audits, and evaluate business issues. In addition, make sure management understands the importance of keeping your department informed.

- *Be aware of all public communications made by your company.* This includes phone directory listings, annual reports, press releases, Internet postings, and marketing materials. These messages may provide taxing authorities with information contrary to what you have indicated on registration forms or audit inquiries, and may even thwart efforts to win tax incentives and audit negotiations.

- *Stay on top of product or business changes.* When your company enters a new market, it may trigger new collection responsibilities. Enhancing services for existing products may also have sales and use tax implications.

(b) Know Your Own Business

To evaluate the sales and use tax impact of certain decisions, it's important to understand *all* aspects of the company's business, stresses Yetter. After becoming familiar with state sales and use tax regulations applicable to your business, take a walk through your facilities to determine if certain processes, items, or materials might be eligible for exemptions that could have been overlooked.

Sales and use tax liability can also be lessened by creative ordering practices. For example, what if tractors purchased by the manufacturing department for use in the manufacturing process are nontaxable, whereas tractors bought by the inventory department are taxable? If older manufacturing tractors are still usable by the inventory department, it makes good business sense to transfer them to inventory as needed and only order new tractors through the manufacturing department, where the purchase is nontaxable.

(c) Use Contacts in Other Departments

One of the best ways to gather information is to make allies in the various departments, says Yetter. Make sure these allies have a basic understanding of sales and use tax as well as a grasp of the importance of their own role in the company's sales and use tax compliance process. Allies in the sales, accounting, credit, requisition, and purchasing departments are extremely useful. She also suggested making friends in the following key departments:

- *Engineering.* The employees in this department who requisition purchases know what they are buying, but you do not. Teach them how to provide adequate product descriptions so accurate tax determination can be made. If possible, incorporate a taxability status indicator on the purchase order form. This way, engineering employees can indicate an item's taxability and accounts payable personnel can make the appropriate tax entries.

- *Marketing.* This department creates the company image. It issues press releases and handles public communications concerning company activities. With an ally in marketing, Yetter says, you'll stay abreast of information before it is made public.

- *Legal.* This department already should have some knowledge of sales and use tax issues, so that it can deal with audit defense and complex taxability decisions, Yetter says.

- *Information systems.* The information systems or MIS department is a key player in sales and use tax administration, warns Yetter. It will participate in any tax automation project, for example, and will generally assist in gathering information for return preparation and audit defense. If the MIS staff is familiar with sales and use tax issues, they will make sure that changes or proposed changes to the computer systems will appropriately address the applicable sales and use tax requirements.

- *Production/plant/operations.* Because the people on the front line understand how the business actually works, they play a crucial role in determining the taxability of items purchased (and sold). Their assistance is very helpful, not only for audit defense, but also for making tax determinations that affect return preparation.

Remember, the making of sales and use tax liability determinations is difficult enough without management and other employees working against accounts payable in this very important task.

Don't let ignorance of sales and use tax issues on their part make your job harder—help them to help you.

(d) Want to Learn More about Sales and Use Tax?

Various sources, accessible via various media, can help with sales and use tax questions and problems.

(i) Conferences

www.salestaxinstitute.com

www.amanet.org

(ii) Newsletters/Publications

www.bna.com

(iii) Software

www.taxware.com

www.vertexinc.com

www.salestax.com

25A.12 INDUSTRY-SPECIFIC SUT ADVICE

No accounts payable professional who has been through a sales and use tax (SUT) audit would describe it as a fun experience. The word *nightmare* might be more applicable. The best defenses for such an experience are knowledge, preparation, and a good offense. Since much of the difficulty of the audit experience is universal, generalized audit strategies can be a great resource for all types of businesses looking to protect their interests and limit their liability during an audit. Helpful as they are, however, such generalized audit strategies cannot address the industry-specific issues for which you will need to prepare.

Your best bet? Anticipate the auditor's industry-specific focus, says Diane Yetter, president of Yetter Consulting Services, Inc. Speaking at a seminar hosted by the Sales Tax Institute in San Diego, Yetter provided the following overview of sales and use tax audit issues in manufacturing, retail, telecommunications, and retail/wholesale industries.

(a) Manufacturing

1. *Review the beginning and ending of the manufacturing process in your state.* Take the auditor on a plant tour conducted by someone familiar with both the manufacturing process and SUT issues.

2. *Use tax accruals.* Auditors will look at out-of-state purchases, so make sure appropriate taxes are accrued on out-of-state taxable purchases.

3. *Withdrawals of items from inventory for use in a taxable manner are subject to tax.* If items were self-manufactured, tax is usually due only on the material costs, not on labor.

4. *Tax or not.* Nonmanufacturing areas usually are considered taxable, including warehousing, shipping, and receiving; plant manager and production supervisor offices; and production administration.

5. *Find all available exemptions in ancillary production processes.* Packaging equipment and supplies may be considered exempt as part of the manufacturing process, as may research and development or production testing. Some processes may be considered production if they result in a product for sale, for example, waste handling functions such as baling and shredding, if the waste products are sold.

6. *Tax intra-plant transportation.* This is usually taxable but may be exempt if necessary and essential to the manufacturing process (e.g., a crane that moves molten steel from one location to another). Check out how conveyor belts, forklifts, and trailers are taxed. Some original items may be purchased exempt as part of an overall machine, while repair parts are taxable because they are sold separately.

7. *Provide documentation.* If the predominant-test rule applies in your state, when mixed-use equipment is used in both a

taxable and a nontaxable manner, documentation must be provided for the exempt use. Forklifts, packaging equipment, and conveyors fall into this category.

8. *Qualify used equipment.* Equipment used to manufacture or generate electricity used in the manufacturing process may qualify for an exemption, including self-generation equipment such as cogeneration facilities. Another issue to consider is whether power equipment is included in the manufacturing exemption. Step-down equipment may not be exempt because it is too far removed from the production process.

(b) Telecommunications

1. Certain service equipment may be exempt or taxed at a reduced rate, including antennae, wiring, cable, and transmission towers.

2. Various federal and state taxes, like the federal excise tax, may or may not be included in the taxable base, depending on the state.

3. Telecommunications providers may also be subject to various local taxes. Telecommunications may be treated differently than other taxable goods and services.

4. Sourcing of long-distance communications and cellular phone charges may be an issue. Most states use the two-out-of-three rule in taxing telecommunications, but some states use a hybrid of the rule.

5. States vary on the taxing of cellular phones sold at a discounted price below cost. Some require the provider to pay tax on the cost of the phone, while others may require the provider to pay tax on the phone's retail price. Other states treat the transaction as a retail sale and tax the nominal amount charged.

6. Some states may calculate the taxable portion of private line services using a ratio of in-state channel mileage versus out-of-state channel mileage.

(c)   Retail/Wholesale

1. *Document exempt sales.* Auditors will spend a fair amount of time reviewing exempt transactions and related documentation.

2. *Regularly review tax rates charged,* especially if rates have changed or significant local taxation is involved. An error of just a few days may result in significant liability.

3. *Bad debt deductions may be an issue* if the company does not track the debts by state or taxability. Any deductions taken for bad debts require documentation to substantiate the debt write-off.

4. *Issues may arise about the taxability of packaging and miscellaneous materials used in making retail sales.* For example, some states will exempt the bag a customer uses to take new clothing home, but will charge tax on the hanger on which that clothing hangs.

5. *Shipping and handling charges may be taxed differently,* depending on what is included in the handling charge and how the charges are represented on the invoice.

6. *Promotional items mailed into a state may be taxable,* depending on the recipient, method of delivery, and whether the retailer has nexus in the state. Marketing materials are usually taxed, though the delivery of such materials to customers through the mail may not be taxable.

Don't make the common mistake of assuming that the auditor knows more than you about your business. Auditors are accountants, not engineers, manufacturers, or computer technicians. You may have to educate them about your business. Also remember that regulations are just the tax department's *interpretations* of state tax law, so challenge the auditor if you disagree with his or her interpretation of a particular issue (court interpretations are the law). The more knowledgeable you are about your industry, the more compelling your arguments will sound to the auditor. Don't be afraid to speak up should it be required. Yetter's advice is a good first step in that direction.

* 25A.13   AVOIDING A SALES AND USE TAX DISASTER

How seriously does your company take its sales and use tax oversight responsibilities? Hopefully, a little more than Tyco International, whose chief executive has been indicted on charges that he conspired to evade $1 million in sales taxes. Speaking at a recent IOMA/IMI conference, Deloitte & Touche's manager Brian Kelleher recommended three approaches that would prevent such a catastrophe. He spoke about a managed compliance agreement, a reverse sales and use tax audit, and automation.

(a)   Managed Compliance Agreement

Kelleher warns that a managed compliance agreement must be negotiated in advance with the state. He calls it a simplified method for reporting sales and use tax on purchases. Here's how it works:

1. In most cases, the company enters into an agreement with the state for a period for three years.

2. The company should obtain a direct-pay permit from the state and then make its purchases tax-free.

3. Each month the company computes an effective tax rate and then remits to the state the tax based on the computed effective rate.

There are many benefits to this approach. For starters, cash flow is increased; and it minimizes overpayments and underpayment, both of which can cause problems for a corporation. Companies using this approach say that compliance is greatly simplified. They also praise the reduced audit and compliance costs.

(b)   Reverse Sales and Use Tax Audits

As those familiar with the myriad sales and use tax laws are well aware, it is very easy to overpay sales or use tax. The rules are complicated and constantly change, and personnel handling the function often leave. Some of the compliance tools used by corporations are not completely effective either.

Thus, some companies hire outside experts to come in and identify refund opportunities. These same experts will also pinpoint potential areas where the company might have an exposure. In both these cases, the company can take one of two courses of action: either file for a refund, to pay excess taxes owed, or simply fix the problem to ensure future compliance.

Kelleher says reverse sales and use tax audits have three phases: *identify, quantify,* and *secure tax refunds.*

Many companies that handle reverse audits for companies do so for a percentage of the savings. A company that undertakes a reverse sales and use tax audit benefit in several ways. In addition to the improved cash flow, it also receives recommendations to improve compliance and has its staff educated, so mistakes can be avoided in the future.

(c)   Automation

Technology is the ideal solution to nitpicky technical issues. And sales and use tax compliance certainly falls into that category. Several companies have developed software to assist in that endeavor. Some of the products on the market today include: Vertex, Taxware, and CorpSales (a Deloitte & Touche product).

(d)   Additional Resources

Due to the constantly changing regulations, which vary by state and even by county, many accounts payable professionals subscribe to publications to keep them on top of the issue. One of the best-known publications is *BNA's Sales and Use Tax Rates and Forms.* To find additional information about BNA's products go to *www.bnasoftware.com/soft/surfabout.html.*

Those who wish to educate their staff about sales and use tax will find the sessions given by the Sales Tax Institute of great interest. To find out when the next seminars will be given, go to *www.salestaxinstitute.com/.*

(e) Conclusion

How serious an issue is this? Here's what New York District Attorney Robert M. Morgenthau had to say about the Tyco situation. "The state and the city are in a fiscal crisis. For someone who was so highly paid to fail to pay over a million dollars in sales tax is a serious crime. There will be zero tolerance in New York for tax fraud and tax evasion, and I hope the federal government will take a similar view." *Managing Accounts Payable* believes that Morgenthau is not alone and that other states will follow his aggressive actions. Is your company ready?

25B

Escheatment (New)

What does your company do about checks that are issued but not cashed? Does it:

- Carry the outstanding checks on its ledgers forever?
- Write off any amounts outstanding to miscellaneous income after six months or a year?
- Turn the money over to the state?

As strange as it may seem to those not familiar with unclaimed property laws, the correct answer in many instances is to turn the money over to the state. Uncashed checks fall under the Uniform Unclaimed Property Act, which requires every company and banking institution to file unclaimed property reports with the states annually, and to make a good-faith effort to find the owners of their dormant accounts. The process is known as escheatment, or simply escheat.

25B.1 WHAT IS ESCHEATMENT?

Every state and county has escheatment after some period of time. While the timing may vary, what is deemed abandoned property—whether tangible or intangible—and is unclaimed by its rightful owner must be turned over to the state or government.

Escheatment then makes it the legal owner to hold the property in a custodial for the rightful owner.

State laws governing unclaimed property dictate that the company must attempt to locate the owner in a procedure called due diligence. If the owner cannot be found during a specified period of time, known as the dormancy period, the property is classified as abandoned. When the rightful owners cannot be found, the money must be turned over to the state.

25B.2   WHAT IF YOU DO NOT ESCHEAT?

States take this law very seriously. The 1995 Uniform Unclaimed Property Act allows penalties up to $25,000 plus 25% of the value of the property for willful failure to report. Claiming that you were not aware of the law has not helped companies, as ignorance of the law is not deemed as an acceptable excuse. Companies can be fined up to $5,000 for inadvertent failure to report. A 12% penalty interest is also charged, and states do not waive this. The interest is calculated from the initial date of the obligation, which can be years.

25B.3   DILEMMA

The issue for accounts payable professionals is to make sure that their companies are turning the money over to the state as required—but not one penny more than they must. This is easier said than done. Here is why:

- *The states are becoming more aggressive in their audit and collection approaches.* There are reports that some states are working together. One auditor may actually represent two, three, or more states.
- *The amounts of money involved are staggering.* Experts estimate that states are currently holding $11 billion with another $2 billion being escheated every year. This is believed to be only a small portion of what should be turned over.

- *Not all uncashed checks have to be turned over.* If those checks represent duplicate payments, which the payee recognized and did not cash, the money does not represent an unclaimed payment. However, the company has to be able to prove this factually. They cannot simply tell an auditor that they believe the check represents a duplicate payment.
- *Money has to be turned over to the state where the intended recipient is believed to reside.* Thus, most companies will find they are responsible for escheating to many states.

Rules as to what has to be turned over and when vary by state. Do you have a headache yet?

25B.4   WHAT CAN BE DONE?

It is not clear where the responsibility for escheatment should lie with the organizational structure. Is it a tax, legal, accounts payable problem—or what? Here are four different approaches used to handle this issue:

1. The entire function falls under the accounts payable department.
2. Unclaimed property reporting to state authorities is currently handled by the legal department, based on information provided by the accounts payable department.
3. The function is handled in the accounts payable department. If funds have to be turned over to the state, the tax department actually handles the processing of forms and the filing. However, the accounts payable department is responsible for cutting the check.
4. The bank administration department handles the function. This department is actually under the umbrella of the treasurer's sector.

Many companies manage their escheat process using software called Freedom Tracker. It helps the company manage the entire escheatment process.

25B.5 NECESSARY DOCUMENTATION

For starters, every company should have a formal escheatment policy. It should clearly state who does what. As can be seen from the above scenarios, escheatment is not an issue that falls solely in the lap of accounts payable. It is likely that tax, legal, treasury, and other parts of accounting may be involved in the process. Which areas handle escheatment vary from company to company. In virtually all companies, however, accounts payable is involved as the department generally provides the check information.

It is important to keep every scrap of paper that might be of use in defending against an escheatment claim by the state. Thus, if a letter is sent out asking a vendor about an uncashed check and the supplier has replied that the money is not owed, the letter and the envelope it was received in should be saved. The reason for this is that they may be needed at a later point to support a claim that a particular check is not subject to escheatment laws.

25B.6 SOFTWARE SOLUTIONS

As indicated, escheatment is an issue that can be handled with software. To even begin to try and complete the forms and track the information manually could be a nightmare. Several states offer simple forms that can be used and even transmit information electronically. However, these are on a state-by-state basis.

A much more attractive solution is to use software that covers all the states. One such solution is available from a company called The Freedom Group. Although most of this company's products are devoted to the insurance industry, its escheatment product can be and is used by companies in many industries. The product is called Tracker 2000.

Tracker 2000 is a software package available for tracking and reporting unclaimed property to the states. Each state requires abandoned funds to be reported annually. Each has different dormancy periods, aggregate levels, and reporting formats. Tracker 2000 keeps track of due diligence requirements and provides a link to Microsoft Word to create search letters. It will:

- Report on the amount of unclaimed property associated with each state.

- Create search letters to send to owners to inform them of unclaimed property.

- File reports on paper, diskette, or magnetic tape.

- Keep track of specific state information such as property types and dormancy values, reciprocal agreements, and contact persons for each state. For more information about this product, point your browser to *www.freedomgroup.com.*

25B.7   OTHER SOURCES OF INFORMATION

Escheatment is a complicated and serious topic. Information, unfortunately, is not widely available and changes as each state modifies requirements or reporting periods. Information can be obtained from each state. Many have this information posted on their Web sites. There are also two companies that offer escheatment services. They are:

1. RECAP, Inc., is a company that specializes in post-audit reviews and has expanded its services to include escheatment. It can be reached through its Web site at *www.recap-inc.com.*

2. Record Time can be reached at 512-345-0291.

As states look for alternative sources of revenue, escheatment as well as sales and use tax have become bigger issues. If a company does not have a good escheatment policy in place, a dialogue should be begun about the issue and a policy established. This is not an issue to ignore.

25B.8   IS IT A BIG DEAL?

It has been a surprise for many to learn that Bankers Trust paid $50 million for failing to escheat. This case, unfortunately, illustrates all the things that can go wrong when a payables department fails to follow proper escheatment procedures. Just before the news broke, Bob Metzger talked about escheatment at RECAP's Enhancing Accounts Payable conference. Given the timing, his advice could be of great use to accounts payable managers who are questioned by their bosses about the proper techniques in avoiding the same problems.

25B.9   WHAT CAN ACCOUNTS PAYABLE PROFESSIONALS DO?

There are several types of properties that are escheated. They include customer or client property, shareholder property, vendor and employee payments, and property due you. Vendor payments are most likely to fall into your lap. Metzger has some excellent advice for managers faced with this issue:

- Start with your bank reconcilement and uncashed checks.
- Review your policy on stop payments, voids, and reversals.
- Find out if outstanding checks are really due to payees or if payees were "made whole."
- Prepare and send payee notifications.
- File with the appropriate states and governments.

This information should be shared with your credit department as well. Corporations are supposed to escheat credit balances since they represent unclaimed property. Not all companies are aware of this requirement.

25B.10   WHAT IF YOU HAVE NOT BEEN ESCHEATING?

Do you now realize that your company should have been escheating but has not done so? The penalties for this can be quite severe. However, not all is lost. In early 2000, a number of states have amnesty programs. Without revealing your company name, investigate whether your state is involved in such a program. This is an issue that should be discussed with your boss and probably the company's legal counsel.

If your state does not have an amnesty program, the discussion should focus on whether to go to the state and reveal your omissions. Many states will treat with leniency those who come forward on their own.

The Bankers Trust case has served to bring a long-ignored accounts payable issue to the forefront. Accounts payable professionals who follow Metzger's recommendations can take the lead within their own organizations and push for adequate escheat policies and procedures. Metzger can be reached at *metzger@recapinc.com.*

25B.11   A PROFESSIONAL ORGANIZATION FOR UNCLAIMED PROPERTY OWNERS

Some reading this are probably thinking that the states get this money and hold onto a good portion of it forever. Those thinking this are correct. There are two professional organizations involved in the escheat process. One focuses on the property holders and the other on the owners. Each has a Web site. They are:

1. *www.unclaimed.org*
2. *www.uphlc.org*

25B.12   AMNESTY PROGRAMS

Recognizing that many companies were not escheating out of ignorance, many of the states ran amnesty programs in 1999. Companies were able to come forward and pay what was owed under the escheatment laws without paying any of the normal penalties. Whether this will happen again in the future remains to be seen. Accounts payable professionals looking for information about such programs in the future can check the two Web sites mentioned earlier and the individual state Web sites. Several publications, including *IOMA's Report on Managing Accounts Payable,* publish this information when they become aware of it.

As states search for ways to generate revenue without increasing taxes, escheatment sticks out like a sore thumb. Politicians would much rather raise state funds by going after companies that the public believes have unlimited funds than increase taxes on the very citizens who have the ability to vote them out of office. Therefore, it is more important than ever that companies follow appropriate escheatment procedures.

25B.13 TYPICAL COMPANY'S UNCLAIMED PROPERTY EXPERIENCE

Unclaimed property is supposed to be turned over to the state. Each state has different guidelines and requirements, making the process difficult for accounts payable professionals whose companies operate in or do business with companies that operate in more than one state. To clarify the process and some of the misconceptions surrounding unclaimed property issues, Karen Anderson, a vice president of Unclaimed Property Recovery & Reporting, Inc. (UPRR) and a speaker at IOMA conferences, shared her expertise. Her advice will get even the escheat novice headed down the right path.

(a) How It Begins

Most accounts payable professionals get involved in unclaimed property in one of the following ways:

1. The state sends a notice saying that the company needs to file an unclaimed property report or that the state is sending in unclaimed property auditors to the company.
2. While attending a seminar, they discover that the company has unclaimed property obligations.
3. The firm that recently purchased the company requires its subsidiaries to comply with unclaimed property laws.
4. The company complies with all applicable laws, including escheat.

Whatever the cause, accounts payable professionals often find themselves thrust into reviewing unclaimed property obligations with little warning.

(b)   Background

As most accounts payable professionals are well aware, escheatment is a requirement that all unclaimed property be turned over to the state. The specifics of when and how vary from one state to another. Included in the definition of "unclaimed property" are uncashed checks and credit balances. After an uncashed check sits on the books for a period of time, some companies pocket the funds, writing it off as miscellaneous income. This money should be turned over to the state in a process referred to as unclaimed property or escheat.

(c)   Going through the Escheat Process

For those who have no unclaimed property procedures in place, getting started can seem like an overwhelming task. Anderson recommends a very methodical approach, delineated in Section 25B.14, "An Unclaimed Property Game Plan." She has also prepared a breakdown by state of the minimum due-diligence amount and the dormancy periods by state.

(d)   Other Important Facts

Anderson points out several other useful facts such as:

- Forty-one states have fall deadlines. The remaining nine states have spring deadlines.
- Accounts payable professionals can expect more audits as state governments look for ways to generate income.
- Accounts payable professionals should also be aware that many firms are performing audits for several states at the same time.
- Never volunteer extra information during an audit. Give the auditors the documents they ask for and nothing more.

There is no reason to give them ammunition for an audit for a different state.

(e) B2B Exemption

Many in the field were counting on the much-ballyhooed "business-to-business exception" to take care of the problem. Readers should be aware that the states call this the vendor-to-vendor exception. It is based on the theory that outstanding balances between two business partners actually represent a duplicate payment or that the difference has been taken care of in a separate transaction. Under this explanation, it would not be necessary for companies to turn the unclaimed property over to the state.

Here's what happened. Nine states—Illinois, Iowa, Kansas, Maryland, Massachusetts, North Carolina, Ohio, Virginia, and Wisconsin—have enacted legislation enabling the business-to-business exception. "But," warns Anderson, "there are very few situations where it actually applies." Why? Anderson explains that the difficulties arose in the ruling of *Texas v. New Jersey.*

In simple terms, this ruling found that if one state (Texas) does not require the unclaimed property to be turned over, then another state (New Jersey) can demand, under its guidelines, that the property be turned over to it.

Anderson says that the only time a professional can feel safe in not escheating is when the transaction involves two companies in a no-escheat state, and neither has responsibilities to escheat to any other state. For most readers, this ruling negates the business-to-business exception. If you have more detailed questions about the specifics of your company's situation, UPRR advises companies on appropriate escheat procedures. Karen Anderson can be reached at 212-971-3333 x24 and via e-mail at *kanderson@uprrinc.com* or by visiting their Web site at *www.uprrinc.com.*

25B.14 AN UNCLAIMED PROPERTY GAME PLAN

Once a company decides to get serious about unclaimed property, it needs to develop a set of policies and procedures for the process.

Anderson has provided the roadmap below, which will also be useful to those already complying if they wish to review their current procedures.

Step One: Assess the Situation

- Review past compliance. Has the company ever reported unclaimed property? If so, what, when, and where?
- Has the company ever been subject to a state unclaimed-property audit? If so, what were the results and what states were part of the audit?
- Are there any subsidiaries to be included?
- Has the company made any recent acquisitions that should be included?

Step Two: Determine Eligible Property

- Does your company have some of the property types covered by most states? These include:
  - vendor checks
  - payroll checks
  - customer credits
  - refunds
  - gift certificates
  - common or preferred stock
  - long-term debt
- What states are represented among the names and addresses to be reported?
- If this is an initial filing, what about years that may not be on the books?

Step Three: Perform the Due Diligence

- What due diligence is required by state? Specifically, focus on:
  - the minimum dollar amount

- timing
- method
- content notice
- What about operational due diligence? This might include developing a strategy to minimize unclaimed property liability and reviewing potentially reportable items.
- Prepare the due diligence letter. This should include the following important elements:
  - response deadline
  - identification number and amount
  - property type/reason
  - instructions for claiming

Step Four: Prepare Reports and Remittances

- Identify due dates for states.
- Prepare a cover sheet with signature.
- Use the proper media (paper, diskette, etc.).
- Use the proper report format.
- Include the remittance (check, wire transfer etc.).

Step Five: Filing Reports and Remittances

- File on time to avoid penalties and interest.
- Get extensions in writing. Only some states will grant them.

Step Six: Follow-up and Reconcilement

- Reconcile general ledger to detail.
- Reconcile paid items to appropriate accounts/divisions.
- File any necessary holder reimbursement claims with the states.
- Establish a filing system for reports and work papers.

Step Seven: Celebrate

Part Eight

Fraud

28

Check Fraud

p. 325. Insert at end of chapter:

28.17 PAYMENT PITFALLS: THINGS YOUR BANKS *MAY NOT* HAVE TOLD YOU (NEW)

All accounts payable professionals are aware of the need to protect their company against check fraud. Speaking at the New York Treasury Management Association's annual Cash Exchange conference, AT&T's Maureen E. McMahon and Bank of America's Nicholas F. Alex revealed that even those who think they have closed all the loopholes might not be as safe as they would like.

McMahon and Alex are part of the Association for Financial Professionals (AFP) Payment Advisory Group (PAG). Its mission is to monitor, interpret, and report on changes to payment systems and the effects of those changes. In addition, the group promotes best practices in payments. The vulnerabilities uncovered were as a result of the work of the PAG.

(a) Liability-Shifting Contract Provisions

The bank is liable for check fraud unless:

- The customer has not exercised "ordinary care."
- The customer has not reported the fraud in a timely manner.
- The customer's employee fraudulently endorsed the check.

Banks have found a way to shift this liability, however—and customers accept it, often unintentionally. Banks often give their customers bank contracts that contain a clause something like: "The bank shall have no liability for its actions under this agreement unless the bank's conduct shall have constituted willful misconduct or gross negligence." On the face of it, this clause may seem reasonable, but anyone who knows anything about check fraud will see the problem. The speakers indicated that in some cases companies might have more rights without a bank contract.

The speakers recommend, first, that a corporate attorney review all bank agreements, paying special attention to liability provisions; and second, that the attorney research whether liability has been shifted from the bank back to the company.

(b) Account Reconciliation Responsibility

The way most companies uncover check fraud is through the bank account reconciliation. The speakers recommend daily reconciliation of accounts. This uncovers questionable transactions such as money laundering activity and expired stops.

Not everyone realizes that stop-payments expire after six months. Some unscrupulous individuals will try to cash a stopped check after the six-month window. Thus, it is important not only that a check be stopped but also that it be removed from the positive pay file. Then, even if the crook tries to cash the check, it won't match and the bank will bounce it.

Another reason for daily reconciliation, point out the speakers, is that when check fraud occurs, it tends to happen repeatedly in a short period of time. Daily reconciliation allows the company to nip this activity in the bud.

(c) "Holder in Due Course" Loophole

Many people do not realize that a stop-payment does not protect a company 100% of the time. The exception is when a person who is a holder in due course presents a stopped check. Despite losses suffered by companies as a result, the rights of a holder in due course have a long legal history and are upheld by UCC Article 3.

The most common example of this is a check-cashing service that accepts a check not knowing that it was dishonored or fraudulent. Because the check cashing company is a holder in due course, it can recover the amount of the check from the issuing company. The payee is liable—if he or she can be found and has sufficient assets—but at this point there is no protection for the company. The process of revising UCC Article 3 began in April of 2000, however, and the AFP will recommend that changes be made to close this check fraud loophole.

(d)   Duration of Stop-Payments

Many people are surprised to learn that stop-payment orders do not last forever. Legally, an oral stop-payment lasts 14 days; one given in writing lasts six months. The six-month period can be extended. Several in the audience noted that their bankers gave them more than 14 days on oral stops. The speakers recommend that:

1. Written authorizations be given to back up any and all oral stops.
2. Stopped checks be removed from the paid issuance file used for positive pay.
3. Attendees use electronic systems for issuing stops if their banks offer the service.

(e)   Stale-Dated Checks

Some professionals thought that their stop-payments protected their companies because banks did not cash stale-dated checks (over 180 days). According to the Uniform Commerical Code, however, a bank can pay a check after a stop-payment order expires in six months, just as it may pay a stale-dated check if it acts "in good faith." Thus, the recommendation is that stop-payments be extended in writing after the expiration of the six-month period. The speakers also noted that a bank will always cash certified checks.

* 28.18   CHECK FRAUD: SAFEGUARDING A/P THE POSITIVE PAY WAY: WHAT'S AVAILABLE NOW AND WHAT'S COMING FROM YOUR FRIENDLY BANKER (NEW)

Most accounts payable professionals know that positive pay is the best defense a company has against check fraud. Unfortunately, the crooks know it as well, and some have found ways to work around it. But this has not stopped the fraud prevention professionals, who have devised ways to make positive pay work. Here's an update of what's available now and what you can expect in the near future to help in your company's battle against forged checks.

(a)   The Problem

Speaking at an IOMA/IMI Accounts Payable conference, a representative from the Bank of America shared some statistics, which demonstrate just how big the exposure is. In 2000, close to 50 billion checks were written. In the same year, there were 30 billion electronic payments. This was broken down as follows:

- 50 percent credit card
- 28 percent debit card
- 22 percent ACH

Here's where the issue becomes problematic. In 2001, 290.8 million paper transactions were converted to electronic ones. The most common of these occurs at the checkout. A consumer pays by check; instead of taking the paper check, the cashier takes the information and converts the payment to an electronic format. The consumer sees a debit on his or her account just as though the check had cleared the account. However, no paper check passed through the system. Thus, if the person writing the check had put a stop payment on it, the item still would have flown through the system. Stop payments don't catch this type of payment.

You may be thinking, "That's interesting but it really doesn't affect my company." It could. Here's how: A fraudster who has your checking account number could initiate such an electronic transaction using your company's bank account number.

In the past, companies often did not worry too much about check fraud, as their banks typically took care of the losses. However, as check fraud began to grow exponentially, it no longer was feasible for banks to cover these losses as an ongoing cost of doing business. Laws were changed, and companies are now liable if it can be determined that they did not exercise ordinary care. The regulations that cover these issues are:

- UCC3 for ordinary care
- UCC4 for reasonable notification
- UCC4A for acceptable security procedures
- Reg CC for shortened return/hold times
- NACHA for unauthorized entries return

Moreover, state statutes may have some wage and labor law restrictions, and union contracts, in some instances, limit options.

(b)   Basic-Positive Pay

To help companies with these problems, banks first developed a product known as positive pay. Here's how it works:

1. Each time there is a check run, the company sends its bank a check issuance file. The file contains only the dollar amounts and the corresponding check numbers.
2. The bank then matches the checks issued or cancelled against those that have been presented for payment and those they are paying against your company's account through back-office processes.
3. When the bank identifies exception items, sometimes called *nonmatches*, it notifies the company.
4. The company then makes a pay or return (dishonor) decision on each exception item by the preagreed-upon deadline each day.
5. A party, preauthorized by the company, must communicate this decision in a prearranged manner. Typically, companies

also decide in advance whether to pay or return checks automatically if the bank has not been contacted by the pre-arranged deadline. It is vitally important that your company monitor this situation and make back-up arrangements when the person responsible for making this decision is absent or unavailable.

(c)   Teller-Positive Pay

Crooks have quickly found flaws in the positive-pay system. They either present the checks in person for cashing at a teller's window or change the payee only. While in the past they may have been able to take a legitimate check made out to John Smith for $10 and change it to one made out to Jane Doe for $10,000, positive pay limited their flex room. They now could only change the payee and were stuck with the same lousy $10—unless they were bold enough to go into the bank to cash the check.

While you may not be bold enough to go into a bank and try to cash a forged check, most forgers are willing to take this risk, or pay someone a small fee to do it for them. Teller-positive pay puts the information at the tellers' fingertips. Now, if your company uses teller-positive pay, when the crook shows up at the teller's window, he or she is informed that the bank is unable to cash the check at this time, and the payee is either referred to the maker (your company), or the bank may try and call to get an approval.

With teller-positive pay, crooks are once again limited to the original amount of the check.

(d)   Positive Pay: The Next Generation

Check fraud has not been abated, though fortunately banks have developed a number of products to further limit the opportunities for check fraud. Here's a look at some of the leading-edge techniques that will be available in the near future. Only the first one is currently available.

- *Online imaging.* This gives the company the opportunity to view the check presented for payment before making the pay or return decision. Both the front and the back of the check can be viewed.

- *Payee name verification.* This is the most exciting development, and may make a serious dent in check fraud. With this product, still in development, the payees' names are included with the data sent to the bank. Now, altering the payee's name will cause the check to reject. The product still has a few kinks. It has certain font restrictions and won't work with manually written checks.

- *Teller line payee name verification.* This product takes the very best features of all the positive-pay products and incorporates them into one hard-to-beat product. Again, there are still some issues to be worked out with the payee name feature.

- *Real-time updates to teller lines.* With this product, there are no delays. The moment a bank receives its download from a customer with the latest check issuance data, the information is available to tellers.

(e) Other Solutions

Of course, one of the easiest ways to prevent check fraud is not to issue checks at all. Obviously, this is easier said than done. However, companies concerned with this issue are starting to make a big push for ACH payments and, where appropriate (payroll, T&E reimbursements, etc.), direct deposit payments. The reason direct deposit is critical is that often the checks that are forged are payroll checks.

Finally, some companies that are switching to electronic payments are using ACH blocks and filters. For example, a company that issues checks might block ACH transactions on checking accounts. This prevents a crook who manages to get hold of the company's checking account number from initiating an ACH debit against the account. This would backfire if someone with a legitimate check tried to convert it at a checkout, but normally, corporate checks are not used for this type of payment.

When selecting checks, it is strongly suggested that you do not always choose the lowest bidder. Saving a few cents on check printing could be costly in the long run. Make sure that a number of safety features, such as microprinting, waved lines, void panatagrams, and others are included in your checks.

29

Employee Fraud

p. 326. Insert after second paragraph:

29.1A   WHAT CAN GO WRONG (NEW)

There are a number of ways that an enterprising employee can confiscate some of his or her employer's money while working in the accounts payable department. Here are several examples:

- A company pays for goods or services received by employees or outsiders.
- A company pays invoices a second time, under a kickback arrangement.
- Vendor invoices are altered and photocopied to conceal alterations. The payment benefits the employee or a third party.
- Check signatures are forged.
- Improper check requests are submitted and the funds appropriated.
- A check is issued for the benefit of an employee or third party and changing the payee in the disbursement journal conceals the misappropriation.
- Bank reconciliations are changed or concealed.

- "VOID" notation eradicated from signed check and the check is then cashed by an employee.
- Kiting to conceal the shortage of funds in a bank account.

29.1B   STEPS TO PREVENT CASH FRAUD (NEW)

Checks and balances are key to preventing cash fraud. By making it more difficult for one employee to divert cash and cover it up, a company reduces its chances of being hit by an employee intent on committing fraud. The separation of duties makes collusion necessary to commit the fraud. While this does happen, it occurs in a significantly lower number of cases than where weak controls make it possible for one person to succumb to the temptation. One person acting alone commits most of all cases of cash fraud.

Besides the losses your company may suffer should cash fraud occur, you have one other strong reason to make sure it does not happen on your watch—it makes you look bad. An accounts payable manager who runs a department with weak policies and controls should not be surprised to be blamed should cash fraud occur in the group.

When the money is gone, especially in cases of cash fraud, it is nearly impossible to get it back before management starts looking for a culprit to blame. What better candidate is there than the manager responsible for the department? Additionally, there is the risk of guilt by association.

To avoid the embarrassment and even worse of having cash fraud occur in your department, institute all appropriate controls, segregate duties wherever possible, and follow the steps listed below. This will minimize the chances of one of your staff members defrauding the company.

1. Checks should be prepared only when receipt and approval is documented, that is, the three-way match has been successfully completed.
2. Supporting documents cancelled to prevent resubmission should reference check number.

3. Insist that check signers review all accompanying documentation before signing checks.

4. Check signers should not maintain accounting or cash records.

5. Signed checks should not be returned to the preparer or requester. They should be mailed to the payee.

6. Voided checks should be cancelled and retained in a separate file.

7. Checks should be issued and recorded in the pre-numbered order. The sequence should also be accounted for when doing the bank reconciliation.

8. Unused checks should be kept under lock and key and accounted for in a log. Access to the locked checks should be restricted to authorized personnel.

9. Bank statements and cancelled checks should be received and reconciled separately from the check writing and recording function.

10. The check signer should review account distribution.

30

Vendor Fraud

30.2 CON ARTIST VENDORS

p. 336. Insert the following in subsection (b), following the words "What can the company do?"

(b1) Pay for Life (New)

This scam is ingeniously simple. A check shows up for $3.50. Most companies do not have the time to research a small check like this and simply deposit it and put it in a suspense account to be applied at a later date. That later date rarely ever comes and eventually the amount would be written off to miscellaneous income. However, the fine print on the back of the check—which is both tiny and in light gray ink, making it next to impossible to decipher—indicates that by cashing the check you are agreeing to pay the payor of the check $29.95 per month—forever.

Why would anyone agree to that? No one would—if they took the time to read the fine print on the back. The trouble is that few people do. Complicating the matter is the fact that the check might show up in a department other than accounts payable, where it is deposited, and the later invoices elsewhere—usually accounts payable. Worse still, some companies will pay small-dollar invoices rather than take the time to verify each one because it is not cost effective for them to do this. Thus, some companies may be paying these crooks without even realizing it.

Should you find yourself in such a position, having cashed one of these checks, all is not lost. One company refused to pay and when the crook started squawking, it simply suggested that the matter could be discussed with the attorney general or the Better Business Bureau. That put an end to the discussion.

p. 337. Insert at end of chapter:

30.3   VENDOR PROFILE FORMS (NEW)

A growing number of leading-edge companies have begun setting up vendor verification programs. Not only do these initiatives discourage fraud, but James B. Arnold, JBA Consulting's chief executive officer, believes they also minimize the number of *relationship* vendors. Arnold told Association of Certified Fraud Examiners conference attendees how to set up a vendor verification program.

(a)   Creating a Vendor Verification Program

"As the custodian of the disbursement process," says Arnold, "accounts payable is in the best position to screen vendors either prior to entry in the vendor master file or once they have reached a given spending level." Thus, it is imperative that accounts payable professionals be actively involved in the establishment of a vendor verification program. They can be the missionary who gets such a program established, if they work with management, internal audit, and purchasing.

The creation of a vendor verification program permits the company to:

- Ascertain that vendors represent bona fide business entities.
- Make sure that vendor selection is based on obtaining the best value consistent with specifications for quality and services.

- Minimize risks from defective goods and services, company reputation, and financial loss.
- Receive appropriate value for purchased goods and services.

(b) What Is a Vendor Profile Form?

Arnold recommends using a vendor profile form to authenticate vendors. While the form is designed to elicit information, it actually discloses telltale signs of the vendor's legitimacy as an ongoing reputable concern. It should request:

- The business name
- Federal employer identification number
- Business type
- Whether the company is Small Business Administration (SBA) certified
- Contact name for negotiation and billing inquiries
- Phone number and e-mail address
- Remittance address
- Physical business address

Arnold recommends that companies include a request for "proof of existence." He suggests that vendors be asked to submit two documents from a list of credible documents. Acceptable proof might come from a Dun & Bradstreet report, city/county business license, or stock certificates.

Arnold advocates that the vendor profile form be sent and returned completed by all vendors before they are added to the master vendor file. He realizes that many companies will not find it feasible to send vendor profile forms to all existing vendors. However, he strongly advises insisting that new vendors complete the form. If they do not, he says, cease cutting checks to them.

(c)   Computerized Techniques

Even if no formal vendor verification program is established, accounts payable professionals can use online services to confirm the authenticity of new (and suspect existing) vendors. By matching the information provided by the vendor against reliable external sources such as Dun & Bradstreet, the accounts payable professional can determine whether the vendor is a legitimate business. "At a minimum," says Arnold, "you will learn if you need to do further background checks." JBA is located in Greensboro, NC.

As one last check, accounts payable professionals can take the phone number provided by the vendor and check it on one of the several reverse phone book sites on the Internet. However, be aware that many of these sites are not frequently updated so legitimate new businesses will not show up.

Insert before page 338:

Part Nine

The New Accounts Payable (New)

Accounts payable is no longer the place where profitable companies dump employees who have not worked out in other departments. Smart management now realizes that the efficient running of an accounts payable department can save their companies thousands, if not millions, of dollars every year. That is why these innovative firms are starting to pay decent salaries to those innovative professionals who run accounts payable.

After all, as can be seen from the previous material covered in this book, accounts payable is more than simply getting a bill and writing a check. In this section, we take an in-depth look at the professionalism that is taking place in the field. It evaluates some of the hiring trends and provides a list of resources that accounts payable professionals can use to educate themselves and their staff. We have included a list of organizations that offer conferences and seminars related both directly and indirectly to the accounts payable function.

The second chapter in this section investigates the salaries currently being paid to the professionals in the field. It also looks at the wide variety of titles being given by corporate America to those who work in the field. The numbers come from the latest *IOMA Accounts Payable Survey* and reflect gender, educational, and experience differentials.

The last chapter in this section is called "Success Stories." In it, we relate the experiences of some of the accounts payable professionals who have achieved exceptional results without extraordinary resources. These are individuals who have looked around at their limited resources and have found ways to improve their lot and the productivity of their departments. They are truly inspiring.

31

Professionalism in the Field

p. 343. Insert new section:

31.6A   ADVICE FOR GETTING APPROVALS ON ALL YOUR A/P PROPOSALS (NEW)

Why do some accounts payable professionals have a much greater success rate than others when it comes to getting approval for projects? "Because," says Frank Sundstrum, Mobil Chemical's assistant controller, "they understand the game plan and know how to influence their boss." He suggests that those who wanted to improve their batting average should:

- *Present your proposal in the language of business—money.* Don't focus on improved efficiency, morale enhancement, error reduction, or any of the issues that are important to you. Mention these items, but translate them into cost savings. That's what management wants to hear.

- *Make management take notice.* If your A/P projects have not resulted in bottom-line savings, include purchasing in your proposal. This will give you the volume you need to get recognized.

- *Know your corporate environment.* Sundstrum says there are actually six or seven different types, but provides the following two broad distinctions: Glitz and glamour versus a shoestring operation. Readers probably already know into which group their company falls; keep this in mind when making your proposal. Sundstrum gives the example of making a proposal for a spiffy new reception area. Glitz and glamour companies would readily consider such a proposal, whereas the shoestring folks would not—unless it resulted in a financial saving.

- *Allow time for acclimation.* Sundstrum gave the example of trying to get a raise for one of his staff. Let's call her Amy. Sundstrum knew his boss would not go for it, so he planned carefully; when Amy helped him complete a successful project that was important to his boss, he mentioned that she had done a great job. That's all he said at that time.

- *Plant the seed.* The next time Amy helped him, Sundstrum mentioned to his boss that he did not know what he would do if she left. Again, that was all he said.

- *Water the seed.* Once again, he mentioned in passing that Amy had done something outstanding to help the department. By the time Sundstrum actually asked for a raise for Amy, there was no argument. It was approved without discussion.

- *Use vignettes to sell your idea at the acclimation or planting-the-seed stage.* Share success stories at other companies. Let's say you want an Internet site for your accounts payable department. You go to a conference and meet a speaker from another company who has installed one. When you come back, share the story with your boss, not forgetting to mention the cost savings. If you work at a glitz and glamour company, you might throw in something about the prestige this gives the other company.

- *Plan, plan, plan.* Obviously, from the examples given here, Sundstrum is an expert at planning. "Even if you can't do long-range planning," he says, "at least take five minutes before you go into your boss's office to strategize."

Sundstrum concluded with one last message: He warned attendees that it was important to focus on the boss's needs rather than their own. He gave the example of a boss who appeared to be against promoting from within. After analyzing the situation, Sundstrum realized that this boss was concerned about having vacancies within the department. Once he realized the problem, he became more creative when recommending in-house promotions. By filling the vacancies created from within the company, he was able to get several people promoted; he then filled the last slot with a temporary worker he had wanted to make permanent. When presented with a plan that did not disrupt the department, the boss gave immediate approval for all the promotions.

p. 346. Insert new section:

31.10   A/P IN THE TWENTY-FIRST CENTURY (NEW)

As corporate America looks for ways to cut costs and increase productivity, the accounts payable function is changing. In just a few short years, it will not look anything like it does today. In fact, looking back on the last ten years, we find a completely different accounts payable function. What does this mean for today's accounts payable professionals? Here is a list of how the function will change and the implications for those wishing to remain in the field.

1. Accounts payable will continue to work closely with purchasing in many organizations. In fact, in some, accounts payable and purchasing will report to the same person. When this happens, it is often the purchasing manager who heads up the new department. What this means for accounts payable professionals is that they had better find a way to get along with purchasing, if that relationship is currently weak. It is too late to mend the relationship the day it is announced that the purchasing manager will now be your new boss. At a recent conference, the speaker projected that in five years, approximately one quarter of all accounts payable departments would report to purchasing.

Many in the audience disagreed, with most believing the number would be higher.

2. Accounts payable work will become less transactional and more analytical as companies look for ways to automate certain parts of the function and eliminate paper. Ultimately, as much as we don't like it, this will translate into fewer, but higher-level jobs in accounts payable. The fact that these positions will be higher level is good news for those who remain. But some, especially those who process payments, may lose their jobs. This is unpleasant news, but it is likely to be the reality.

3. If some accounts payable professionals lose their jobs, they will inevitably be forced to find new ones. As the job market gets more competitive, employers will start, as so many have already, to demand a college degree. While your current employer may recognize the fact that you are doing an excellent job and not care about the lack of a degree, a new boss is not likely to be so understanding. Many companies use the lack of a degree as a way to weed out candidates if too many apply for a job. My advice to those who do not have a college degree is to go back to school. This can often be done at night and sometimes with your current employer footing the bill.

4. The big news in the twenty-first century may be that the departments will finally start to go paperless. What was once a pie-in-the-sky dream is actually starting to come true in many organizations. While e-mail, imaging, and workflow got the ball moving, electronic invoicing just may be the resource that gets the paper out of accounts payable. In a recent survey, close to half the accounts payable associates responding indicated that their companies were either already receiving invoices over the Internet or intended to do so over the next two years. Productivity concerns boosted by the anthrax mail threat just may push many companies in that direction. Learn everything you can about the process and the companies offering the service.

31A

Salary and Titles
in Accounts Payable
Today (New)

Individuals active in the accounts payable field today are experienced, well educated, and, in a growing number of cases, earn an enviable salary. With close to 550 professionals participating, the latest IOMA survey gives an accurate picture of the state of the industry. Specifically, accounts payable managers are earning more than $50,000 on average, have 16 years experience in accounts payable, and really three-quarters have a college degree or higher.

31A.1 OVERVIEW

The two dominant accounts payable positions are the manager and the supervisor, at 34% and 23%, respectively. Accounts payable coordinators accounted for 17% of those responding. Exhibit 31A.1 shows the average salaries by gender of those participating in the survey.

The emergence of the director title in relationship to accounts payable is an encouraging sign. Although we have seen the title sporadically, the fact that close to 4% of those responding had this

Exhibit 31A.1 **Average Salary by Title**

	Men	Percentage of Title	Women	Percentage of Title
Senior management	$72,381	$84,231	0.62	$53,125	0.38
AP director	$73,947	$77,000	0.53	$72,500	0.42
AP manager	$51,643	$58,565	0.31	$48,554	0.69
AP supervisor	$40,229	$45,577	0.11	$39,567	0.89
AP coordinator	$33,397	$35,833	0.08	$33,143	0.9
Analyst/specialist	$33,100	$35,000	0.1	$32,889	0.9
Accountant	$36,042	—	0	$36,042	1
Other	$41,170	$55,769	0.28	$35,588	0.72

Source: IOMA.

title is a good sign for a profession looking to improve its image. Even more encouraging is the fact that another 8% had titles normally associated with senior management. These include vice president, controller, treasurer, and assistant controller. The significance of the inclusion of these titles is that corporate America is finally starting to recognize the importance of the accounts payable function.

Several other pictures emerge when the data are examined further:

- The "higher" ranking the title, the larger the percentage of males at that level.
- Males earn more than females at virtually every level.
- Not only is the accounts payable profession dominated by females, but at the supervisor level and below, it is almost entirely female.
- While men may earn more than women at all levels, the pay gap has narrowed considerably at the director level. This is good news as this is a fairly new title in most organizations and those who attain it are almost as likely to be female as they are to be male.

31A.2   COMPANY SIZE AND INDUSTRY

In general, the larger the company, the higher its pay scale is likely to be—at least if you hold the title of accounts payable manager. The only exception in our study was for males employed at mid-sized companies with 200 to 499 employees. These employees actually earn more than anyone else in the title does. The pay disparity between males and females is substantial at those companies with fewer than 500 employees.

There is not much pay difference for female accounts payable supervisors. They all earn very close to $40,000. Exceptions lie in those companies with 200 to 499 employees in which the average pay is slightly above $35,000. Surprisingly, the group that pays its male accounts payable managers so well pays its male accounts payable supervisors poorly. It should be noted when looking at the breakdowns for male supervisors that there are very few males in this title so the numbers are not overly meaningful.

For a complete breakdown of the salary information by title and company size, see Exhibit 31A.2. Exhibit 31A.3 shows the breakdown by industry and gender. Since there are so few males with the accounts payable supervisor title, the gender breakdowns are not meaningful when spread over so many different categories and therefore are not shown.

Exhibit 31A.2   **Average Salaries for Accounts Payable Manager and Accounts Payable Supervisor by Size of Company**

	Accounts Payable Manager			Accounts Payable Supervisor		
	Avg. Salary	*Men*	*Women*	*Avg. Salary*	*Men*	*Women*
Up to 199	$43,365	$57,500	$40,795	$39,250	$35,000	$39,722
200–499	$49,479	$63,929	$43,529	$35,357	$27,500	$36,667
500–999	$51,354	$53,889	$49,833	$39,352	$31,250	$40,000
1,000–4,999	$53,274	$58,889	$49,063	$42,672	$55,000	$40,700
Over 5,000	$58,214	$62,273	$55,588	$45,833	$75,000	$40,000

Source: IOMA.

Exhibit 31A.3 **Average Salaries for Accounts Payable Manager and Accounts Payable Supervisor by Industry**

	Accounts Payable Manager			Accounts Payable Supervisor		
	Avg. Salary	*Men*	*Women*	*Avg. Salary*	*Men*	*Women*
Manufacturing	$54,113	$62,368	$50,465	$42,083	$57,500	$40,682
Financial/ banking	$51,932	$57,727	$46,136	$46,667	$65,000	$43,000
Wholesale/ retail/ distribution	$47,391	$49,000	$46,944	$35,000	$27,500	$35,625
Private practice firms	$48,854	$45,625	$49,500	$32,786	$36,250	$31,400
Utilities, communication, transportation	$58,864	$66,667	$49,500	$50,833	$50,000	$51,071
Nonprofit	$42,862	$55,000	$38,007	$42,500	$35,000	$45,500
Education	$49,286	$45,000	$50,000	$38,333	—	$38,333
Health care	$53,000	$68,333	$49,167	$35,893	—	$35,893
Hospitality	$51,667	$51,667	—	$34,286	$27,500	$35,417

Source: IOMA.

31A.3 WORK EXPERIENCE AND EDUCATION

IOMA also took a look at the effect experience has on earnings. Female accounts payable managers have slightly more overall work experience and accounts payable experience yet earn more than $10,000 less. While male supervisors have two years more overall experience, they have slightly less accounts payable experience, yet earn approximately $7,000 more than their female counterparts. See Exhibit 31A.4 for a complete breakdown of salary information by work experience.

Exhibit 31A.4 Average Salary for Accounts Payable Manager and Accounts Payable Supervisor by Average Years Experience and Average Years Accounts Payable Experience

	Average Overall Experience		Men		Women	
	Avg. Salary	*Avg. Yrs. Exp.*	*Avg. Salary*	*Avg. Yrs. Exp.*	*Avg. Salary*	*Avg. Yrs. Exp.*
A/P manager	$51,601	15.9	$58,177	15.4	$48,880	16.1
A/P supervisor	$40,523	13.7	$47,083	15.6	$39,711	13.5
	Average A/P Experience		Men		Women	
	Avg. Salary	*Avg. Yrs. A/P Exp.*	*Avg. Salary*	*Avg. Yrs. A/P Exp.*	*Avg. Salary*	*Avg. Yrs. A/P Exp.*
A/P manager	$51,848	6.9	$59,133	6.4	$48,661	7.1
A/P supervisor	$40,915	6.4	$47,083	5.7	$40,128	6.5

Source: IOMA.

So, you are thinking, it must be education. Men are better educated than women are, you say. Not accounts payable women! While a few female accounts payable managers have not attended college, 65% have either a college degree or a master's degree. Exhibit 31A.5 shows the breakdown of salaries by level of education and gender.

Exhibit 31A.5 **Average Salaries for Accounts Payable Manager and Accounts Payable Supervisor by Level of Education**

Accounts Payable Manager

| | | | Men | | Women | |
Education Level	Avg. Salary	%	Avg. Salary	%	Avg. Salary	%
High school	$43,333	5.2	—		$43,333.3	100
Some college	$43,050	23.6	$52,500	19.5	$40,758.6	80.5
College degree	$53,643	60.3	$58,393	40.0	$50,476.2	60.0
Masters/MBA	$63,421	10.9	$72,500	21.1	$61,000.0	78.9

Accounts Payable Supervisor

| | | | Men | | Women | |
Education Level	Avg. Salary	%	Avg. Salary	%	Avg. Salary	%
High school	$41,364	9.4	$35,000	9.1	$42,000.0	90.9
Some college	$37,148	37.6	$55,000	4.5	$36,297.6	95.5
College degree	$42,547	45.3	$44,643	13.2	$42,228.3	86.8
Masters/MBA	$39,722	7.7	$45,000	33.3	$37,083.3	66.7

Source: IOMA.

Education does not appear to have a big impact on the salary levels of accounts payable supervisors. In many cases, extra education does not appear to improve one's earning capacity in this title. Given the low number of males with the supervisor title, we have not shown the gender breakdowns.

Exhibit 31A.6 combines the education and experience factors. While males with some college have more overall and accounts payable experience than might partially account for the pay discrepancies, the same is not true for those with more education. The numbers are most revealing for those with college degrees. Not only does this group have the largest number of responses, women in this group have more work experience than men in the group—yet they still earn less. The comparison for those with advanced degrees is even more startling.

Exhibit 31A.6   Average Salaries for Accounts Payable Managers by
Level of Education and Experience

| | Men | | | Women | | |
Education Level	Avg. Salary	Avg. Yrs. Exp.	Avg. Yrs. A/P Exp.	Avg. Salary	Avg. Yrs. Exp.	Avg. Yrs. A/P Exp.
High school	—	—	—	$43,333	17.9	7.6
Some college	$52,143	24.0	13.9	$40,001	17.3	9.5
College degree	$58,500	15.1	5.2	$51,404	15.4	6.2
Masters/MBA	$72,500	10.0	3.8	$61,154	16.8	6.5

Source: IOMA.

31A.4   BONUSES

Yes, some accounts payable professionals do receive bonuses. The average bonuses paid by title are included in Exhibit 31A.7. Over one quarter of those with the title accounts payable managers received a bonus that averaged $6,272. However, only 9% of those with the supervisor title received this added compensation, which averaged $3,045.

Exhibit 31A.7   Bonus

	Average
Senior management	$14,813
AP director	$9,251
AP manager	$6,272
AP supervisor	$3,045
AP coordinator	$2,314
Analyst/specialist	$1,900
Accountant	$8,500

Source: IOMA.

Management is starting to recognize the contribution accounts payable professionals make to the corporate bottom line. The fact that senior level titles are now being bestowed on those responsible for the accounts payable function is a good sign for a profession that is viewed by some as being little more than clerical.

Throughout this report, we have pointed out certain pay inequities related to gender. There are many reasons why this exists. Partial explanations of this phenomena include:

- Men tend to work at larger companies that pay better than smaller ones.
- Men are more aggressive in asking for pay increases and not taking no for an answer.
- Men may have already pursued a strategy of having the grade level of their positions increased.

Given the wealth of information that today's accounts payable professional is required to know, higher grade levels for the job should be investigated at all companies that have not done so in the last few years. To help readers with that daunting task, a high-level human resources executive explains how they should go about the process.

31A.5   HOW TO HAVE A/P POSITIONS REEVALUATED FOR GRADE-LEVEL CHANGES

Most managers face the issue of what to do with staffers at the top end of the pay range. To help answer this question, accounts payable professionals should realize that there is great flexibility in salary ranges. Despite what it says in the personnel manual, in many companies it is no big deal to pay someone more than the high end of their salary range. It is done all the time. Before embarking on a campaign to have the job level or grade raised, determine if the grade restrictions are simply being used as an excuse not to pay a higher salary. If that is the actual case, you will be wasting valuable time and subjecting yourself to a lot of needless stress by trying to have the grade level raised.

Assuming that is not the case, realize that bosses will benefit by the accounts payable function being raised in grade level. The reason for this is quite simple. The higher the grade level of the people reporting to a boss, the higher his or her level can be. By pushing to have the accounts payable department's jobs raised in grade level, the accounts payable manager may be indirectly benefiting the boss.

Once you have decided to push forward, begin by performing a review of the function and the accounts payable professional's performance. Document any actions that have saved the company money, reduced costs, or earned the company money. The review should also cover any new responsibilities you or the department has taken on. Many people who have been in the same job for more than a few years have gradually taken on more responsibility without ever having a change in title. Consider what the job entailed when it was first taken on and what it encompasses today and include all enhancements in the review.

By documenting any progress and discussing the situation with your boss, you will find that perhaps you can have your job levels and your associated compensation raised. Once the manager has successfully done this task, the rest of the positions within the department can be similarly reviewed. Accounts payable has come a long way from the days when all accounts payable did was write checks to pay invoices.

31A.6 TITLES

It is time for corporations to take a long, hard look at the titles for accounts payable professionals. Many have completely inappropriate titles that hinder supervisory efforts to have pay levels increased. The proper title is the first step to securing adequate pay. It also goes a long way toward ensuring that the accounts payable professionals are afforded the respect they deserve from the rest of the company.

(a) The Problem

The author receives frequent calls from accounts payable professionals whose companies want to upgrade their positions but do not know where to begin. "What titles are other companies using?" is the common theme of these calls. The matter was open to debate on the accounts payable discussion group (*www.ioma.com*). Here is how one company handled this issue:

"We have done several things in my department. Currently, my accounts payable person is called an 'accounts payable coordinator.' However, in January we are reorganizing, and there will be two employees doing accounts payable, and one doing T&E. My two accounts payable employees will become payables associates, and my T&E person will become a T&E associate. My current title is payables manager. I chose 'payables associate' because my accounts payable and T&E people do much more than just processing. They each have their own reconciliation and are responsible for several other tasks. I also feel that associate is a more meaningful title, and helps employees to think of our department as a real customer service environment. This way, they know that we are here for them."

Another company differentiates its accounts payable positions as follows: "We use accounts payable clerk as our title for invoice processors, and we also have a file clerk whose main duty is filing. I am the accounts payable supervisor. You should contact your human resources department for job titles and descriptions. My human resources department has reference books with this type of information and they will not change a job title unless the duties are significantly changed as well."

Another accounts payable professional reports that "We call our accounts payable clerks 'accounts payable bookkeepers' because they reconcile GL accounts. This can be extremely complex due to the number of subsidiary companies that the parent corporation pays."

(b)   Approaching Human Resources

As indicated earlier, the way to change titles is to work through human resources. This should be done only with the approval of the accounts payable department's immediate supervisor. Often, the human resources department will not have a clear idea of an employee's many responsibilities. Therefore, it is a good idea for supervisors from both departments to meet and resolve that situation. Before this meeting, make a comprehensive list of everything done, and try not overlook anything—no matter how insignificant you feel it may be. Petty cash, sales and use tax, escheatment, 1099s, value-added tax (VAT), duplicate payment procedures, automated clearinghouse (ACH), electronic data interchange (EDI), and purchasing cards should all be included. Do not forget things like recommendations for process improvements, and past accomplishments with, if possible, cost savings. Only when they have this information firmly in hand can human resources properly do their job.

(c)   Recent Trends

Given all the advances of technology and the use of purchasing cards, small invoices are disappearing from the corporate structure. This frees the accounts payable manager to make process improvement recommendations and participate in other corporate activities.

Some companies are now using the term *disbursements* instead of accounts payable, so they have a disbursement manager instead of an accounts payable manager. All the titles discussed later in this chapter may also be altered to accommodate this change. We see no advantage or disadvantage to such an approach—it is simply a personal preference. However, those who feel accounts payable has a bad reputation within their companies might consider the change.

(d) Suggested Title Structures

IOMA constructed the following list which shows a possible structure for an accounts payable department:

- Accounts payable clerk/coordinator/bookkeeper
- Accounts payable associate/specialist/analyst
- Accounts payable supervisor/assistant manager
- Accounts payable manager
- Accounts payable director
- Vice president—accounts payable

If your company has less than six people in its accounts payable department, you may eliminate some of the suggested levels. For the skeptics viewing the list, yes, we have seen a number of accounts payable professionals at both the director and vice president level—with salaries to match the title.

31A.7 CERTIFICATION

There has been much discussion in the field about the lack of a certification program for accounts payable professionals. The IAPP has been investigating the possibility of establishing a program and has tentative plans to begin one in the fall of 2000. As we go to press, this has not been formally announced. Check the *www.iappnet.org* Web site for updates on this pressing issue.

32

Success Stories

p. 361. Insert at end of chapter:

32.4 CASE 4: HOW ONE MANAGER USED TECHNOLOGY TO IMPROVE THE ACCOUNTS PAYABLE DEPARTMENT (NEW)

Three years ago, the accounts payable manager at Charles Schwab faced the now standard productivity issue of how to find ways to get more work done without adding staff. The reason? A new system had left the group with a backlog and the department's image badly needed to be spruced up. Today the Schwab accounts payable department is productive and enjoys a first-class reputation within the company. At the IOMA/IMI Accounts Payable conference, Daniel Parnas, Schwab's director of corporate accounting, explained how this metamorphosis took place.

(a)   New Millennium Challenges

"Accounts payable," says Parnas, "is a thankless job. No one pats you on the back or thanks you for a job well done." He concedes that changing an image takes time. Schwab's main challenge was to support future growth without adding staff and find ways to improve productivity while maintaining employee morale, maximizing productivity, preserving exceptional quality, and sustaining excellent customer service.

To meet the goals set by management, it was clear that technology had to play a key role. Parnas strongly advises all accounts payable professionals to constantly stay abreast of the latest developments in technology. He also suggests periodically reevaluating existing technology not currently being used in their operations. "What did not work in the past," he says, "may work today."

(b) Technology Selection

There is no one right solution for all companies. At any given point, says Parnas, certain techniques will be considered leading edge. Although p-cards were considered quite impressive a few years ago, a large number of companies that began using them lost some of their distinctiveness. Currently, the Internet and imaging are the glamour stocks of accounts payable world.

Parnas recommends selecting a technology solution that will not only work in your organization, but one that will fall within your budget. He provides a list of potential technology solutions for accounts payable.

Using the 80/20 rule, Schwab discovered that 80% of their invoices were for $5,000 or less. Negative assurance is being used on those invoices. The next big focus for Schwab is the Internet.

(c) Right Solution

Parnas advises accounts payable professionals to look at their business needs. He strongly suggests performing a cost benefit analysis. Do it even if your company does not require it. This will not only improve the chances of having your technology solution approved, but it will also enhance the image of the accounts payable manager.

Do not look just at available technology but also at alternative solutions. If money is an issue (and when isn't it?), Parnas suggests looking at older technology that costs less.

Also take into account industry characteristics. He gives the example of evaluated receipt settlement (ERS), which may be a great solution in a manufacturing environment but is not an appropriate choice for Schwab.

Corporate culture and senior management focus will play a key role in the chosen solution. If management does not listen to accounts payable, find an ally in the information technology (IT) department. Look for infrastructure support and consider partnering with IT.

A joint project can accomplish a number of objectives in one fell swoop. You can improve the accounts payable department's productivity, as well as the relationship with IT. Support for your proposal from the IT department will go a long way toward getting the needed approval. In the process, the accounts payable department's reputation will go up a few notches.

(d)   Making the Change a Success

The strongest way to change the department's image is to identify key measurements and monitor these indices. Put the measurements in a report, graph the results, and share them with both the staff and management. Implement these measurements for continuous feedback. Benchmark these results and look for best practices.

One of the best ways to identify leading-edge processes is to get out of the office and talk to peers at other companies. Accounts payable professionals can accomplish this by attending conferences or meetings of professional organizations.

Any new process improvement will benefit from front-end planning and organization. By taking the necessary amount of time you will succeed at taking on this new initiative.

Finally, communication is crucial, not only with management but also with your staff. A monthly meeting is a good way to make sure the staff is kept up-to-date. It also gives the staff an opportunity to ask questions and air issues that might be on their minds. Parnas recommends breakfast meetings for those accounts payable departments that cannot spare the time during the day.

Accounts payable professionals will continue to be challenged to get more work done with fewer resources. Parnas was

100% on target in identifying technology as the best way to effectively meet that goal. Accounts payable professionals who heed Parnas's advice will be able to emulate his remarkable success. According to Parnas, some technologies now being used in accounts payable departments include:

- Interactive voice response
- Imaging and workflow
- Electronic travel and entertainment (T&E)
- Corporate intranet
- Electronic data interchange (EDI)
- ERS
- Electronic funds transfer (EFT)
- Procurement card
- Internet

32.5 CASE 5: BENCHMARKING AND MEETING MANAGEMENT'S OBJECTIVES (NEW)

Faced with the challenge of improving accounts payable operations and not sure where to start? Told by upper management to cut staff or costs with no advice on why or how? At the recent IOMA/IMI Accounts Payable conference, Owens & Minor's Charlie Winnagle described in detail how he benchmarked his department and met management's objectives.

(a) Background

Owens & Minor is a national distributor of medical supplies. It had a decentralized operation with 88 full-time accounts payable team members processing 1.8 million accounts payable transactions each year. Hampered by a legacy system developed 10 years earlier, the department also had a year 2000 (Y2K) problem that was to be solved with a new client/server enterprise-wide system.

Winnagle was given a senior management mandate to centralize the company's accounts payable operations concurrent with the installation of the new system. He was told this new operation could not have more than 40 employees. World-class benchmarks for accounts payable showed each full-time employee processing 51,000 invoices annually, and this was the O&M target.

(b)   Was the Change Necessary?

Needless to say, the task Winnagle faced was monumental. Given the management directive, there was no doubt that he would attempt to meet their targets. Additionally, he says, the process that was in place was completely out of control with both paper and the number of hours being worked continually increasing. But there was an even bigger incentive for the group to change; the company was missing $750,000 a year in lost cash discounts.

The Y2K issue and an existing system that did not support a centralized accounts payable department were further incentives. Finally, the senior management request for the reduction in General & Administrative expenses (G&A) made it impossible to continue as they were.

(c)   Where to Start

Winnagle began by developing some common measurements of his current process. He looked at the number of invoices processed in accounts payable each year, the cost to process an accounts payable invoice, and the number of invoices processed each hour.

When all the numbers were calculated, Winnagle discovered that his operations were all over the board. His employees processed anywhere from 15,000 to 48,000 invoices each year. He had his work cut out for him. He also began a search for accounts payable benchmarks. He examined a number of them, including:

- KPMG, the public accounting firm known for its benchmarking data of large companies
- The Internet

- Trade organizations, including IOMA and National Association of Procurement Management (NAPM)
- Finance trade publications including *Controller Magazine, Management Accounting, Journal of Working Capital Management,* and *CFO* magazine

(d)   Research Results

Winnagle found a good deal of information including a 1995 article in *CFO* that offered a lot of useful advice and useful statistics. While Winnagle was not pleased with O&M's standings, the results were not bad. Yet, O&M was not satisfied.

The results for his different locations were all over the place. His best location was processing 33,587 invoices. Another was doing it at a cost of $1.19. On the flip side, his worst location was processing 15,946 at $2.79 apiece. The corporate average was 20,714 at $2.43 apiece. He set an interim goal for his group to have each staffer process 33,587 invoices each year.

(e)   Assessing the Results

Winnagle began by evaluating the numbers from each location. He discovered that three of them were performing significantly better than the others. He looked into what they were doing differently, and the procedures at those three locations were documented. He also investigated adapting the procedures used by the three top producers to the other locations.

He realized that through process mapping the department would be able to reduce the time in the process by 25%. An accounts payable focus group was formed. This facilitated a two-day work session for users and division managers on the "new process" and opened it up for review and discussion.

The consensus of the group was to adopt the new process and benchmarks for the company and establish "O&M's Best Internal Practices." His intermediate goal was to bring the performance of all divisions up to the middle level. In this way, the worst-performing units would be brought to average.

(f)   Results

Initially, there was a three-person reduction, which the company was able to achieve through attrition. He was able to document the procedure changes and distribute this to the organization and get an agreement as to the start date. He also met other goals as follows:

- The centralization of the accounts payable remote locations into one will take place as scheduled.
- The staff reduction to 40 was not met—it was exceeded.
- The goal of 51,000+ invoices per employee was also exceeded. Winnagle expects to hit 55,000.

He was able to exceed the world-class benchmarks by using EDI and Pay on Receipt as enablers. Some readers may know Pay on Receipt as evaluated receipt settlement (ERS). He says that the centralization process has not affected the company's customers. The improved process controls now allow the company to take the discounts previously lost and the Y2K problem has been fixed.

Winnagle is justifiably proud that the staff reduction was able to take place without laying off a single employee. Attrition took care of the problem as well as the fact that certain staffers were picked up by other departments. Finally, he was able to reduce salaries, general and administrative expenses by $1,300,000 annually.

(g)   Accounts Payable and the Bottom Line

What Winnagle showed the attendees at the conference is that accounts payable professionals can make a real impact on their company's bottom line by taking a hard, cold look at their operations and streamlining them to meet management objectives. In this case, benchmarking was just a tool used to identify reasonable goals and organizations doing the best job. Armed with this information, most will be in a position to see more clearly what needs to be done and where improvements can be made. Winnagle's experience shows not only that it can be done, but how to do it.

32.6   CASE 6: HOW ONE ACCOUNTS PAYABLE MANAGER GETS THROUGH YEAR END (NEW)

Due to taxes, closings, and vacations, the worst time of the year for accounts payable managers is year end. In one of the most entertaining sessions at the IOMA/IMI Accounts Payable conference, Genette Howard, an accounting manager at World Minerals, Inc., shared her secrets for coping and successfully getting through this trying time. *Her secret*: Remember to "breathe." For Howard, this has a double meaning. Not only does it mean to take a deep breath before reacting when things go wrong, but it also reminds you of what you have to do. "Breathe" stands for:

> B = basics
>
> R = reminders
>
> E = expenditures
>
> A = accruals
>
> T = taxes
>
> H = help
>
> E = examine

(a)   Basics

The first thing Howard recommends is to determine what the year-end cut-off date will be. Notify all affected departments once this decision has been made. "Set the deadline and then enforce it," says Howard. She also says that there can never be too much communication and everyone should be made aware of the appropriate dates.

It is crucial to have adequate staffing in order to get through year end. Howard recommends a policy of no vacations. "If you let your processors take vacations," she warns, "you will end up processing invoices." She does not believe that this is a smart way to use a manager's time. She urges accounts payable managers to work smarter, not harder.

(b)   Reminders

Howard categorizes reminders into two sections: external and internal. She suggests sending formal closing letters to all affected parties two to four weeks before the cut-off date. She backs this up with friendly e-mails to employees with outstanding items. Similar notices are sent to project managers and those she suspects have outstanding travel expenses. She tracks down employees who have not turned in T&Es by looking over the airline bills to see who has purchased airline tickets but not submitted T&E reports.

She "knows" who is likely to be delinquent: the traveler who has not submitted a report for six months and the employees who tend to submit T&Es for more than one month at a time. Most accounts payable managers know the identity of the T&E laggards at their company.

Internally, within the department, she holds meetings with the entire group so the staff is kept up to speed. At these gatherings, she emphasizes the importance of the rapid processing of invoices. She gets feedback from her team about the workload and evaluates the current status. She emphasizes the importance of teamwork in getting through year end.

(c)   Expenditures

Howard's objective is to get all expenditures recorded in the appropriate period. She includes T&Es, inventory items, and invoices for capital projects in this goal. However, as those who work in accounts payable know only too well, it is never possible to get in everything.

(d)   Accruals

Howard then sets up accruals for the items that are not recorded. She does this for material received but not invoiced, invoiced material that has not been received, and unrecorded travel expenses. She also asks all department heads if they know of any additional expenses that need to be accrued.

(e) Taxes

"Don't forget taxes," she warns. Accounts payable departments are usually responsible for producing 1099s at year end, and many leave this task until the last minute. She reminds accounts payable managers to order the forms early enough. Those who have not done so yet this year should make a note to do so soon. She recommends reviewing the 1099 process before the year-end rush. Because this is done only once a year, many are not familiar with it.

Accounts payable managers should also start getting missing tax ID numbers as soon as possible. Print a trial run so the 1099s can be reviewed before the final run. Most important, Howard says, START IN TIME.

(f) Help

The year's end puts additional pressures on the accounts payable staff. Those once-a-year tasks add up and can sometimes overwhelm even the best-managed departments. Use temporary agencies if the workload gets to be too much.

Another recommendation is to prioritize the work and require overtime, if needed. To minimize the negative effects of requiring overtime, give the staff as much notice as possible if overtime is required. Take a proactive approach.

(g) Examine

Some of the work in accounts payable can be monotonous. When extra tasks are added to an already busy group, the chances for error skyrocket. To prevent this, Howard focuses on examining every facet that affects year end. She frequently examines the workload, the communication level, the attitude of her coordinators, the workflow, and her internal checklists. If anything goes wrong in any one of these areas, Howard says the accuracy of the work her group produces can suffer. And, she says, accuracy is just as important as speed.

Year-end closing requires a team effort. Those who follow Howard's fine advice will find their own year ends flow just a little smoother, *and* they will still be breathing when it is over.

32.7 PPL ELECTRIC OFFERS LESSONS ON SETTING UP AN A/P IMAGING SOLUTION (NEW)

Do any of your accounts payable processors leave difficult invoices for someone else to process? Do they wait until five o'clock to slide problem invoices past their supervisors? Are you sick of piles of paper and rows of filing cabinets? Well, if the answer to any or all of these questions is yes, imaging and workflow may be for you.

Brian Krom, corporate disbursements manager, shared his experiences with implementing an imaging and workflow solution at PPL Electric Utilities Corporation. First, however, is a description of why they wanted to move in these directions.

(a) Why Imaging and Workflow

Krom enumerated seven reasons for moving to imaging and workflow:

1. Processed efficiencies and reduced cycle times. This was accomplished by decreasing paper hand-offs, decreasing or eliminating bottlenecks, eliminating manual date stamping, reducing the delays in routing "trouble" invoices, and saving on labor costs.

2. Improved work distribution through FIFO (first in, first out) processing. Invoices were prioritized within or between queues, and flexibility and control were added over individual image filters.

3. Improved monitoring, tracking, and reporting of the vouchering (workflow) and backlogs. This was achieved through real-time count of processed and pending invoices by operator type, scan date, and the like.

4. Improved document retention, retrieval, and archival.

5. Improved customer service.

6. Improved fraud control.

7. A lot less storage space.

Imaging makes document handling much easier—for example, Krom can now print, fax, or e-mail images directly from within the system. He says that multiple copies of documents are no longer kept, nor are there lost, misfiled, or "out" vouchers. The need to copy and mail paper documents is eliminated, as is refiling.

Krom warns that much of the labor savings throughout the process may be offset by the labor costs for invoice sorting, prepping, and scanning. He also noted that sometimes those real-time reports of pending invoices could be quite depressing.

Imaging and workflow eliminates the need to save papers and keep microfilm/fiche. However, some accounts payable professionals must observe certain rules to meet governmental requirements. Krom summarizes the SEC and IRS rules, but cautions that additional regulations may apply. He points out that it is not required to convert to imaging as your source document, but if you do, you must follow the regulations.

(b)   The Storage Space Issue

Space saving is usually an issue whenever the imaging topic comes up. Krom demonstrated just how much space PPL saves. He says that the accounts payable department fills up 82 filing cabinets each year. Each cabinet takes up eight square feet of floor space (this includes two feet of clearance to open the drawers). That's approximately 650 square feet of space each year. Trying to find something in one of these cabinets is another challenge.

The $5\frac{1}{4}$-inch optical platters used by the PPL accounts payable department each hold 2.6 gigabytes of images. Seventeen are used for each year's information. Next year, Krom plans to upgrade to platters that can hold twice as much information.

(c)   The Implementation

To begin with, PPL developed a business case. Tentative management approval was gained and a vendor was selected that satisfied accounts payable's requirements—as they understood them at the time.

PPL tried to understand the software functionality and tested and experimented with it. PPL spoke with other users and even insisted on talking to the technical staff, in addition to the salespeople. Krom urges others to do the same. He also recommends speaking with other customers of the software vendor.

PPL then mapped out the current process. This mapping was more difficult and took longer than expected, but PPL learned a lot from the process. With the current information under its belt, PPL designed and mapped the new process. When gaps in the process were identified, the company then had to decide whether to change the process or customize the system. Hardware requirements were determined and acquired. These included workstations, server size, scanners, and jukeboxes; along with them came decisions about how much horsepower was needed and what settings and configurations would be used. The software was installed, tested, debugged, and retested. Customizations were implemented. Then, Krom says, PPL tested and tested and tested—and it should have tested more!

The company wisely decided to pilot with a small number of invoices, using one of its smaller affiliate companies first. PPL continued debugging and adjusting the process and software based on feedback from the pilot. It went into full production on January 10, 2000.

(d) Lessons Learned

Krom says it was more difficult to adjust to imaging than he had expected. PPL experienced much resistance from its staff. However, most of these staffers came around fast after using the new system.

The project was more involved and intrusive than assumed, and what was supposed to have been a turnkey solution did not turn out to be so. Although the original start date was projected for October 1999, it was delayed until January 2000. Such delays are not ideal; however, this project came in remarkably close to deadline.

(e)   The Possible Downside

These systems are expensive. The imaging and workflow system at PPL cost just under $100,000. This includes software, mods, hardware training, and installation. The annual maintenance fee is $6,500. For a company like PPL, with huge volume (300,000 transactions per year), this is not a significant cost, although those with smaller volumes might look for a lower-priced system.

More of an issue was resistance to the new project. The imaging and workflow resulted in several significant changes in the accounts payable department and not all of the staff were happy about these revisions.

Scanning is a skill that needs getting used to. If your company deals with many differently shaped and colored invoices, be prepared *not* to receive an exact match.

(f)   Final Thoughts

More time and effort were needed up front for document preparation and sorting. Krom had to add a person to handle the increased workload.

PPL, like many other companies, experienced an invoice-processing backlog during the implementation of the imaging program. Krom concludes that, even with all this, "we have already begun to realize many of the benefits and expect that to continue. It was an interesting road but worth the effort."

32.8   IVR FREES A/P FROM ANNOYING "WHERE'S MY MONEY" CALLS (NEW)

Accounts payable groups being inundated with phone calls regarding payment status will find interactive voice recognition (IVR) systems to be a big help. This was especially true at Hoffman-LaRoche, Inc., where the accounts payable staff had two groups of difficult people—suppliers and their own sales force—demanding to know where their payments were. Speaking at NAPP's conference, Nancy Sampson shared her experiences of IVRs, showing not only the benefits but also what should be expected of IVRs if a company installs one.

(a) Definition

What is an IVR? Interactive voice recognition systems allow people to interact with computers through their telephones. In the Hoffman-LaRoche example, a caller can obtain information pertaining to the expected payment date of certain invoices by entering a series of numbers in response to prerecorded questions.

(b) Background

In 1995, Hoffman-LaRoche, Inc., installed its first interactive voice response unit in the accounts payable department. This was a boon to staff productivity. Suppliers could determine when their payments would be made, and so could the sales staff. This is particularly important at a pharmaceutical company such as Hoffman-LaRoche, because it provides many honoraria to doctors and hospitals. When the salespeople called on one of these people, they wanted to be able to tell that customer when the honorarium money would arrive.

In 1999, the company installed SAP; the existing IVR system was not compatible with SAP and thus was disconnected. Recognizing that this would put a strain on the accounts payable department, the system was replaced by a person to answer questions formerly addressed by the system. This seemed like a reasonable solution. Unfortunately, the vendors and salespeople started calling individual processors, disrupting the workflow of the entire department. Therefore, an SAP-compatible IVR system was quickly purchased.

(c) Overall Objectives

Like many other companies, Hoffman-LaRoche wanted to improve productivity in its accounts payable department. It wanted to:

- Use technology to reduce costs

- Reduce non–value-added work
- Maximize the use of employee time
- Increase the level of customer service
- Provide 24/7 service availability

(d) System Selection

The company reviewed three systems, using three criteria to justify the ultimate selection: cost, efficiency, and compatibility with SAP. The system selected was SAP-certified and had one other big advantage: It had already been installed in the human resources department. Thus, there were cost savings from the sharing of hardware and piggybacking on already-installed software. Finally, the accounts payable department was able to leverage other in-house resources.

The systems evaluated were Edify Electronic Workforce, Syntellect, and CCS.

(e) System Requirements

Sampson demanded certain features from the new system. She required that it:

- Be simple to use
- Have the ability to transfer to a customer service representative
- Allow a letter to be input with three keystrokes
- Be able to expand beyond the current eight lines currently in use
- Have reports available to measure productivity

She was adamant that the ability to transfer to a live person be part of the system, but that this feature not be available at the beginning of the call. The reports feature measured who was hanging up, what questions the suppliers were asking, and the length of time the calls were taking.

(f) What the System Does for Suppliers

A few conference attendees expressed concern about security issues. Sampson assured the group that unless the persons requesting the information regarding payment had the necessary input information, they would not be able to access the data stored on the IVR system. Specifically, suppliers are able to query the system by:

- Purchase order and invoice number
- Invoice number and invoice amount
- Vendor number and invoice number
- Vendor number and invoice amount
- Check number

Only those who are entitled to receive information have the necessary numbers to access the system.

(g) What the System Does for Employees

The company's sales reps use IVR to inquire about promotional expense reimbursements and the aforementioned honoraria. These reimbursements go directly to the sales reps or to third parties for expenses relating to sales promotions.

Once the system was up and running, it was discovered that employees were using IVR to inquire about their T&Es and payroll. These calls are routed to a T&E inquiry group or payroll, as appropriate. Sampson hopes to expand the system in the future to include online capabilities over the Internet.

32.9 HOW ONE PRO TOOK A/P OUT OF THE PICTURE WHEN RESOLVING CUSTOMER DISCREPANCIES (NEW)

Does your accounts payable staff waste endless hours trying to resolve discrepancies with the purchasing department? Jim Heard at Dana Corp. found a great way to solve this problem. The company refers to the mechanism as a trouble board. "The trouble board," says Heard, "is a communication tool between accounts payable specialist and buyers. Since there can be more than one buyer at a plant, there are multiple trouble boards, one for each buyer code on our system." What happens if one buyer uses more than one code? Heard says the company has the ability to combine these into one trouble board to simplify their maintenance of the system.

(a) Purpose of the Boards

If the three-way match were perfect, there would be no need for Heard's trouble boards. However, as those reading this are well aware, there are often discrepancies in the three-way match. The rationale behind the trouble board was to give each buyer hands-on ability to approve an option of payment necessitated as a result of a mismatch of the three-way match. In other words, explains Heard, quantities or prices on the PO are different from those on the invoice. The boards deleted faxes and phone calls to the buyers across the United States and eliminated duplication of handling in cases where the buyer approves invoice quantities and prices.

There are additional benefits to the accounts payable department. The trouble board items do not require additional handling by an accounts payable specialist. "Once the buyer approves the invoice," says Heard, "it is transmitted to Dana Corporate for payment the day after the buyer gives the approval." This entails no additional effort on the part of the accounts payable department.

(b) Approval Different from the Invoice

As those who work in accounts payable know, paying an amount different from the dollar amount indicated on the invoice can create huge headaches at a later date. But not at Dana Corp. "In the case where a buyer approves receiver quantities or PO pricing contrary to invoicing, the system creates a debit memo or credit memo to properly carry out the buyer's decision, but the item is put on hold pending accounts payable specialist handling," explains Heard.

He says that the reason for this approach is the possibility of additional charges needing to be added to the automatic memo to recover freight or taxes that could not be automatically calculated within the system.

(c)   What's Needed to Implement a Trouble Board

While this sounds like a great idea, not every company will be able to implement the model exactly the way Dana Corp. did. "The whole concept of a trouble board," says Heard, "was made possible by the availability of electronic POs and receipts within the system." He says that purchasing employees resisted the change, but after two years, it is well accepted.

There is another reason the trouble boards work well. A tolerance exists within the system that allows the company to place parameters within the system to keep petty discrepancies from hitting the trouble board.

(d)   Future Enhancements

Heard is always looking for ways to make existing processes work better. Another reason for allowing the tolerances was that the boards are plant-specific, not supplier-specific. The variation and mix of merchandise being purchased is best served by a supplier-specific tolerance.

Heard plans to address this issue in the near term, which he defines as within the next three to four years, depending on IT resources. Why so long? "Once a system functions, enhancements such as this takes a back seat to implementations in progress. Over the next year, implementations and enhancements will be hard to come by," he explains.

* 32.10   CASE STUDY: BLACK BELTS RESCUE DELL'S A/P DEPARTMENT FROM A DELUGE OF PAPER (NEW)

Conventional wisdom says just-in-time inventory may be a great concept for a company intent on efficiently managing its stock, but it makes life difficult for the accounts payable department responsible for paying all those just-in-time invoices. Or does it? Consider the example of Dell Computer Company, which found itself ordering certain parts as frequently as 12 times a day. The accounts payable department was inundated with paper invoices. Then a nifty solution was devised for the company by one of its vendors, GE Capital. While GE didn't pocket one cent of the savings it enabled Dell to find, it reckons that the goodwill it generated will translate into additional sales.

(a)   The Solution

GE dispatched several of its Six Sigma analysts known as "black belts" to Dell to analyze its accounts payable process. The black belts mapped out the entire process step by step. When studying the results of this analysis, it became readily obvious, even to those who knew little about accounts payable, that while just-in-time inventory management may have made the purchasing function very efficient, it had directly the opposite effect on accounts payable. The recommendation was that the company change to an Internet-based electronic filing process. Dell estimates that the move saves it $2.4 million per year.

Many reading this have probably heard about Six Sigma but may not understand all its complexities. Those who would like to learn more should go to *www.ge.com/sixsigma/SixSigma.pdf*.

(b)   What Is Six Sigma?

Six Sigma is a highly disciplined process that helps us focus on developing and delivering near-perfect products and services. Why "Sigma?" The word is a statistical term that measures how far a given process deviates from perfection. The central idea behind Six Sigma is that if you can measure how many "defects" you have in a process, you can systematically figure out how to eliminate them and get as close to "zero defects" as possible. Six Sigma has changed the DNA of GE—it is now the way we work—in everything we do and in every product we design. There are three key elements of quality: customer, process, and employee.

(c)   The Customer: *Delighting Customers*

Customers are the center of GE's universe: they define quality. They expect performance, reliability, competitive prices, on-time delivery, service, clear and correct transaction processing, and more. In every attribute that influences customer perception, we know that just being good is not enough. Delighting our customers is a necessity. If we don't do it, someone else will.

(d)   The Process: Outside-in Thinking

Quality requires us to look at our business from the customer's perspective, not ours. In other words, we must look at our processes from the *outside in*. By understanding the transaction life cycle from the customers' needs and processes, we can discover what they are seeing and feeling. With this knowledge, we can identify areas where we can add significant value or improvement from their perspective.

(e)   The Employee Leadership Commitment

People create results. Involving all employees is essential to GE's quality approach. GE is committed to providing opportunities and incentives for employees to focus their talents and energies on satisfying customers. All GE employees are trained in the strategy, statistical tools, and techniques of Six Sigma quality. Training courses are offered at various levels:

- *Quality Overview Seminars*. Basic Six Sigma awareness
- *Team Training*. Basic tool introduction to equip employees to participate on Six Sigma teams
- *Master Black Belt, Black Belt, and Green Belt Training*. In-depth quality training that includes high-level statistical tools, basic quality-control tools, change acceleration process, and flow technology tools
- *Design for Six Sigma (DFSS) Training*. Prepares teams in the use of statistical tools to design it right the first time

Quality is the responsibility of every employee. Every employee must be involved, motivated, and knowledgeable if we are to succeed.

(f) Key Concepts of Six Sigma

To achieve Six Sigma quality, a process must produce no more than 3.4 defects per million opportunities. An "opportunity" is defined as a chance for nonconformance, or not meeting the required specifications. This means we need to be nearly flawless in executing our key processes. Six Sigma is a vision we strive toward and a philosophy that is part of our business culture.

At its core, Six Sigma revolves around a few key concepts (source: *www.ge.com/sixsigma*):

- *Quality*. Attributes most important to the customer
- *Defect*. Failing to deliver what the customer wants
- *Process capability*. What your process can deliver to the customer
- *Variation*. What the customer sees and feels
- *Stable operations*. Ensuring consistent, predictable processes to improve what the customer sees and feels
- *Design for Six Sigma*. Designing to meet customer needs and process capability

* 32.11   E-INVOICING: HOW ONE POWER COMPANY DEVELOPED ITS OWN WEB-BASED PROCESSING SYSTEM (NEW)

As companies everywhere cut back, a growing number are turning to technology to help address the needs of doing more with less. Allegheny Energy was one such company that had to consolidate several accounts payable units into one centralized location and reduce staff by over one-quarter. With employees in many locations, the company had to find a way to facilitate workflow. After examining several commercial packages, the company decided to develop its own Web-based processing system. "We call it Tran$act," says Dave Hovis, the company's manager of payment processing.

(a) Background

Like many companies, Allegheny Energy's accounts payable department needed to provide its employees with the ability to process invoices efficiently, despite the number of widespread areas involved in the process. The company has 6,000 employees in 11 states and was hamstrung by a rather inflexible mainframe accounts payable system. It also used a workflow imaging system. Six years ago, the company centralized into one accounts payable department by reducing the number of accounts payable employees from 32 to 23. Thus it was ripe for the development of an electronic process, which it rolled out in a phased approach as explained in the following steps.

1. *T&E expense reports.* Using the company intranet, employees completed their T&E expense reports. The company required that employees fax copies of receipts to the Right Fax server and then attach statements from Fax to the expense statement. At that point, the report is submitted for approval and then sent to accounts payable where receipts and approvals are verified. The statement is uploaded into the mainframe accounts payable system, and checks are cut or funds are direct-deposited into the employees' bank account. Ideally, employees can complete their statements and have funds in their accounts the following day.

2. *Check requests.* Allegheny Energy uses check requests for payments without invoices. The check request form is completed in Tran$act and electronically routed to the approver and then to accounts payable where proper approvals are verified. The request is uploaded to the mainframe, and the check is cut or the funds are deposited into the vendor's account the following day.

3. *Direct charge invoices.* Allegheny Energy defines direct charge invoices as those small-dollar invoices not associated with purchase orders. Upon receipt, the accounts payable department scans the invoice and routes it electronically to the user for accounting and approval. If the invoice is received in the field, it is faxed to the Right Fax server and then attached by the user to a Tran$act direct charge screen. The accounting is added and the item routed electronically for approval. Once the approval is obtained, the item is directed to accounts payable where the approvals are verified and the taxability reviewed.

4. *Preapproved invoices.* This function is used for utility invoices, primarily telephone, that fall within a preset dollar amount. Upon receipt, the accounts payable department scans these invoices. The dollar amount and account information are added. If the invoice falls within the agreed limits, it automatically pays the next day. If it is greater, it is routed electronically to the appropriate person for approvals. When it is returned, it is paid the following day.

5. *A one-card program.* The company was able to combine its purchasing and travel card programs into one. Once a month, it takes an EDI file from the bank and loads it into Tran$act. All cardholders are then e-mailed their statements. As a default, each card is tied to a single line of accounting. When the cardholders receive their statements, they are responsible for reviewing them and making all accounting changes to reflect appropriate accounting. Using Right Fax, they must attach receipts and route for approval. Accounts payable spotchecks the receipts and the approvals. Payment is made to the bank based on the original EDI file, again using the default accounting. Any changes to the default accounting are uploaded to the mainframe each night, debiting the correct account and crediting the default account. To verify that all the appropriate changes have been made, the system generates a zero-dollar check for this transaction.

(b) Future Enhancements for Service POs

Currently, the company is developing a process that will allow the user to make a receipt for the purchase order in the mainframe through an HTML line with Tran$act. This development will be implemented shortly.

Hovis also says that the system includes real-time validation to the company's PeopleSoft accounting system to ensure proper accounting is used. It also has a duplicate invoice checking process. He says it complements other electronic processes in place, including:

- EDI invoices
- Interfaces with other applications
- Receipt-initiated vouchering
- Spreadsheet uploads for tax payments, wage garnishments, and temporary staff services.

(c) Impact on Accounts Payable

Allegheny has made a serious dent in the manual processing of invoices. To date, from the 426,000 annual transactions, the staff in accounts payable key only 94,000. A remarkable 78 percent of all transactions processing is done electronically. But this does not satisfy Hovis. His goal is 90 percent.

The powerful move to electronics has also paid off in a big way when it comes to invoice processing costs. Hovis says that, in 1997, the cost per transaction was $8.48. Today it is $2.64—a reduction of 69 percent in five years. He has also reduced headcount in the department due to Tran$act and other initiatives. The number of accounts payable staff at Allegheny is now 15.

He credits the staff for a lot of the improvements: "The Tran$act team of people in accounts payable and IT is an extremely talented group that can literally make changes on the fly. These enhance the system according to the needs of our internal customers. I am very proud of the work they have done in delivering a product that far exceeds any commercial product available, at a fraction of the cost."

* 32.12 OUTSOURCING: BUYERS BEWARE: LESSONS LEARNED FROM AN A/P OUTSOURCING EXPERIENCE (NEW)

Do many of the executives in your company think that the accounts payable function is a no-brainer that could easily be outsourced? If so, they might be interested in the experiences of another company that thought exactly the same way. Consultants often advise companies to outsource their "nonstrategic or noncore" functions. While those who work in accounts payable can foresee the potential problems with this approach, management often does not and goes ahead with the outsourcing. Speaking at an IOMA/IMI Managing Accounts Payable conference, Mary N. Birmingham shared Equiva Services's experiences on the outsourcing roller coaster.

(a) Background

Equiva was formed through a joint venture between Shell and Texaco in 1998. It was a quasishared services organization, which handled a huge number of invoices. Invoice processing was decentralized.

Typically, companies outsource to:

- Reduce operating costs.
- Utilize world-class processes.
- Free internal resources for other activities.
- Focus on core competency.
- Allocate resources most efficiently.
- Share risks.

Equiva outsourced to:

- Get expertise from the outside for a commodity-type product.

- Free resources from managing noncore skill set
- Take advantage of best practices in the activity.
- Reduce costs.

The company outsourced the portion of accounts payable that was centralized. This accounted for roughly 12 percent of the total activity. It also outsourced the reconciliation of bank accounts, of which there were a substantial number.

(b)   What Happened?

The performance of the outsourcer, whose experience in the oil and gas industry was not extensive, fell short of expectations. This resulted in an invoice backlog, delayed and late payments, and worst of all, duplicate payments. Additionally, the outsourcer could not drive process improvements, nor could it provide meaningful metrics.

The fact that the outsource provider's work processes were not compatible with the Equiva environment was a point of contention. Like so many others who think that the accounts payable function is easy, the provider had underestimated the skill level required of the employees who perform the work. The ensuing situation was not pretty. Here's what happened:

1.   Vendors became dissatisfied.
2.   The company's image was tarnished.
3.   Accounts were not reconciled.
4.   Internal customers were extremely frustrated.
5.   Other work groups began processing their own invoices.

(c)   Lessons Learned

The company had some hard lessons to learn because of this experience. Clearly, the corporate culture was not ready for outsourcing. Almost as apparent was the fact that management did not recognize the work effort and complexity of the accounts payable function. As many readers will readily acknowledge, the Equiva management is not alone in this view.

Birmingham enumerated several other lessons learned, including:

- The need for a procedure or process for addressing failure to perform
- The need for compensation at a fixed price, which cannot be incentive-driven
- Releasing experienced staff prior to the transition might not have been a wise move

(d)   Taking Action

Recognizing that the outsourcing arrangement was not working, Equiva developed a case for action. It cancelled the agreement with the outsource provider and developed an organization hierarchy of its own. Since its experienced staff had been released, Equiva turned to outside temporary agencies for resources.

Birmingham says they also documented policies and procedures, and when a process did not work, it was changed. To measure the department's progress and performance, metrics were developed and used.

The Equiva experience is a useful lesson not only for those considering outsourcing, but also those whose own procedures have not been reviewed and updated for some time. The action steps Equiva took can serve as a road map both for those who are considering outsourcing and those whose departments might need a review, and perhaps even an overhaul.

Index

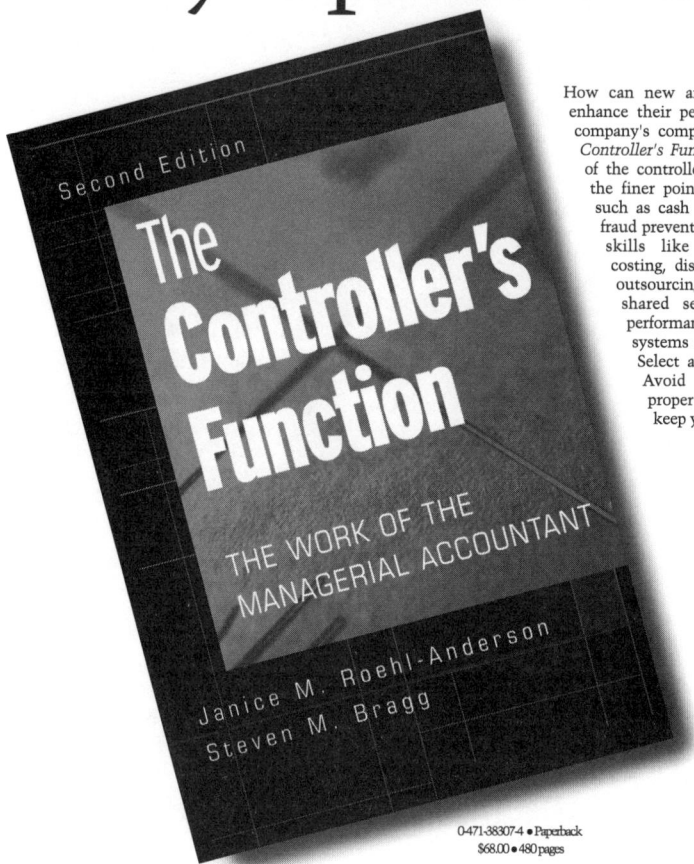

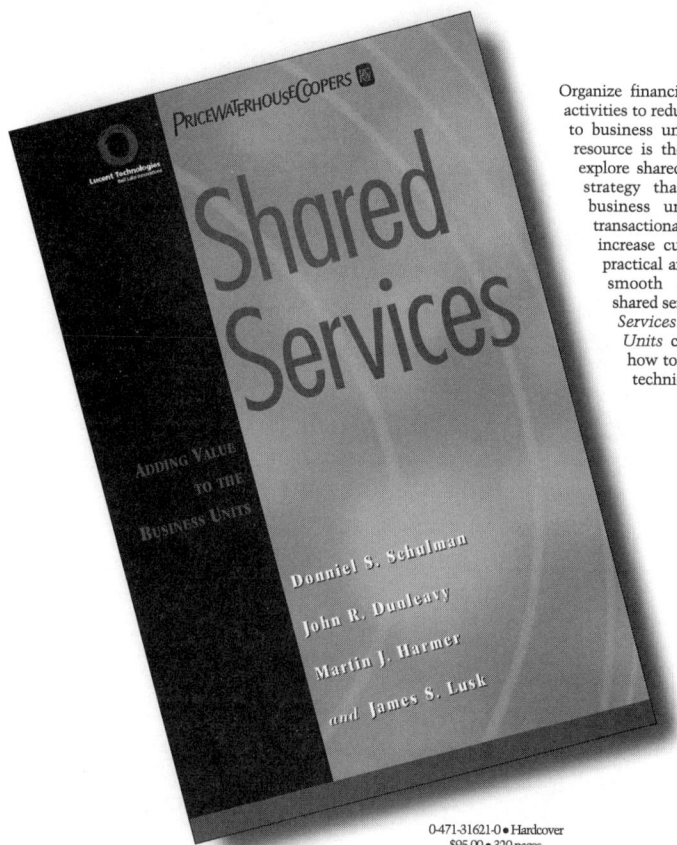